YOURS TRULY

YOURS TRULY

A TRUE STORY OF PROSTITUTION

TALLULAH DEVERE

authorHOUSE®

AuthorHouse™
1663 Liberty Drive
Bloomington, IN 47403
www.authorhouse.com
Phone: 1-800-839-8640

First published by AuthorHouse   06/20/2011

ISBN: 978-1-4567-8580-2 (sc)

Printed in the United States of America

Any people depicted in stock imagery provided by Thinkstock are models, and such images are being used for illustrative purposes only.
Certain stock imagery © Thinkstock.

This book is printed on acid-free paper.

Because of the dynamic nature of the Internet, any web addresses or links contained in this book may have changed since publication and may no longer be valid. The views expressed in this work are solely those of the author and do not necessarily reflect the views of the publisher, and the publisher hereby disclaims any responsibility for them.

This book is a work of non fiction based on the life, experiences and recollections of Tallulah Devere. Names of people have been changed to protect the privacy of others.

This book is dedicated to all the women who have lost their
lives whilst working in the sex industry.
God loves you all.

Acknowledgements

There are a number of people I would like to thank and the first has to be Paul, without your help, support and sense of humour this book would not have been possible. To Adrian, thank you for believing in me, and never standing in judgement. I am blessed to have you in my life. A big thanks to Gerry, for using your red pen as mercilessly as I use my cane. To Uncle Bob, who has always made me feel valued. Thank you to my sons, for standing strong and united in the face of adversity. I'm proud of you both. To Kate, a good friend, I can always have a laugh with. Thank you to my editor, Sarah Cheeseman. And thank you to my partner for your encouragement.

"The books that the world calls immoral are books that show the world its own shame."

Oscar Wilde.

Introduction

I began writing this book shortly after suffering a miscarriage at the age of forty eight. Even though an unplanned pregnancy I was left feeling devastated and alone with my grief. Over the weeks that followed a mixture of anger and pain flooded my senses, so much so I felt unable to function. I gave up work and instead put pen to paper. Over the months that followed the words poured out and I began to heal.

Unlike many books of the same genre this book was not written to make the profession sound glamorous, nor does it portray prostitution as something that always involves drug addicts and the exploitation of young vulnerable women. Although this is a problem in the industry, all the women I met appeared to have a choice. It is a true account of what goes on inside a typical brothel, where women do have choices, and are well paid for their services.

Not enough is said in favour of the brothel but experience tells me a well run establishment provides a valuable and needed service. It also provides a certain amount of protection for the girls in a very dangerous profession. Sex is a fundamental part of being human and men, for whatever reason, should be able to pay for it in a friendly and safe place.

Perhaps one day well run brothels will be accepted and even valued in the UK, but until then they will continue to operate amongst us, like it or not.

Chapter 1

I was woken by a loud knock at the street door. Recently, this had become an all too familiar sound—bailiffs trying to collect on behalf of various creditors. As I wondered what debt it was for this time, my partner stirred.

Oh no, I thought, *please don't wake up until the bailiffs have gone.*

I just couldn't bear the thought of an argument first thing in the morning. My partner blamed me entirely for our dire financial situation, even though, in the two years he'd lived with me, he'd made no effort to get a job. Looking back, I realise I was partly to blame. At the time of meeting him he was renting a pretty shabby room from a drug dealer friend on a rundown council estate in south-east London. After only a few dates I invited him to stay for the weekend at my house in the Kent countryside. He never returned to his life in London. Instead, he began a new one with me. My infatuation for such a good-looking man, who was nine years younger than I, clouded my judgment. I allowed him to take over everything, from disciplining the dogs and the kids, to rearranging the house, and even making him a partner in my antique business—which wasn't even making a profit.

From the day he moved in he began to cost me. I soon discovered he had a drug habit. Looking back, I guess I was naïve concerning puff [hash]. I thought it was a harmless non-addictive drug without side effects. I could not have been more wrong. He was volatile and paranoid, with a violent temper, and would erupt over the slightest thing. But the most difficult thing to deal with was his silent treatment. After an argument he would very often shut himself in the sitting room for days on end, only coming out to use the toilet. Early on in our relationship I would spend hours crying, begging him to come out and have something to eat or drink. I couldn't understand this behaviour, as I'm the type of person that has an argument to clear the air and then make up soon after, so this kind of treatment was absolute torture. Only after reading a psychology book did I realise he was playing a control game and I stopped playing along.

I stopped crying and begging at the door, and didn't offer him food or drink. Instead, I just cooked for myself and the boys. When it came to bedtime I would resist trying to entice him up and retire quietly. Late at night he would raid the fridge, often eating an entire block of cheese and drinking all the milk. Five days passed, and then on the sixth morning, after getting back from the shops, he spoke from behind the closed door asking for a cup of coffee.

Getting back to that morning . . .

'Open the door please, miss,' came a voice through the letterbox. 'Equity Collections here. You may as well open the door so we can discuss matters.'

I knew better than to do that. Once the door is opened, a bailiff can legally enter your property. My house was full of antiques from my failing business. I would rather put the items into auction than let them pick at the pieces like vultures.

I carefully got out of bed, without waking my partner, and walked along the hallway to the window that overlooked the street. Parked in the road was a large white van. Two men in dark grey suits were standing near it smoking and chatting. I strained to hear what they were saying, but with double glazing and a long front garden I couldn't hear them properly. They looked very intimidating with bull necks, cropped hair and huge biceps bulging from beneath their rather strained sleeves—the very image of nightclub bouncers. I dared not move the net curtain for fear of them spotting me. After a few moments, they threw their cigarette butts into the front garden.

One of them went to the van and appeared to be writing something on a card. He then slowly walked up the front path and rattled the letterbox as he posted it. I couldn't help thinking, as he walked back to the van, that he reminded me of a silver back gorilla by his build. Just as the van drove off, my partner got up and went to the bathroom. I ran downstairs and hid the card under some telephone books before he could see it. The bailiffs had visited on behalf of my council tax debt, as I owed two thousand pounds. This was only a small part of my problem, as I was also four months in arrears with my mortgage and was being threatened with court action and possible eviction. My monthly payments had risen to one thousand three hundred. The gas and electric companies were about to install pay-as-you-go meters because I also owed them money. I had agreed to see a man from the mortgage company that same afternoon to work out an affordable amount that I could pay each month to make up the arrears. The fact was, I couldn't afford anything at that moment.

My eldest son, Henry, had left for college before the bailiffs' visit and my youngest, George, was still in bed. I told him to get up or he'd be late for school and made tea for us. I also made a coffee for my partner, who'd come downstairs and gone straight to the computer in the sitting room where he spent most of his time. I suggested he should make himself scarce before the mortgage man arrived, as he'd be more sympathetic to a single mum.

Chapter 2

At precisely two o'clock, as arranged, the mortgage man knocked on the door. As I was expecting his visit I'd just put on some lipstick, and after checking my hair in the hallway mirror I opened the door to a large, friendly looking gentleman who introduced himself as Peter. I showed him into the dining room and asked if he'd like tea or coffee.

'Yes please, tea would be lovely, two sugars and milk. Then come and sit with me so I can help you draw up an income and expenditure account.'

I found a few digestive biscuits in the cupboard, put them on a plate and popped everything on a tray.

'Right, now, young lady, let's get some figures on paper. What are you earning at the moment?'

'Nothing, business is very bad.'

'Well, love, we need to show something to the big boys at Head Office.'

I'd already worked out my monthly outgoings the night before and now passed the piece of paper over to him. After a few moments, he took off his glasses and looked straight at me.

'I'm going to be honest with you, love. The mortgage company you're with is like a loan shark, and if you don't start paying off your arrears now they'll start court proceedings to have you evicted. From what I can make out you still have equity, and it would be a shame to see that go.'

'But surely I'd get that money back if they repossess and then sell the house.'

'The trouble is the mortgage company is only interested in getting its money back quickly. Therefore, it would put the house up for auction, and as long as it reaches the reserve, they're happy.'

'Oh, I didn't realise that. What do you suggest I do?'

'You could always go on the game,' he replied.

I expected him to laugh, but he didn't. Instead, he was looking at me earnestly.

'Don't be silly, I'm too old.'

'Not at all, you're a very attractive lady.'

'Are you serious?' At this point I didn't know whether to be flattered or offended.

'Do you honestly think I could do it?'

'Why not? I've a couple of lady friends that do, and they're a lot older than you.'

'But how would I get customers?'

'Put an ad in the free local paper. You know, the one you can pick up at supermarkets and petrol stations.'

I was beginning to feel embarrassed and uncomfortable talking to him and decided to change the subject back to the mortgage debt.

'Peter, how can I stop them repossessing my house?'

'You will have to start making your monthly payments of one thousand three hundred plus an extra two hundred a month to pay off the arrears.'

'There's just no way I can pay that much!'

'Well, as I said to you earlier, darling, if you don't make the payments they will repossess. And very fast! Anyway, I must get going now as I have another client to see. Here's my private mobile number if you want to talk about anything. Nice meeting you. Good luck and take care.'

I put his business card in my pocket and thanked him as I showed him to the door. After he left I sat thinking. What kind of job was going to pay my debts? With no recognised qualifications I couldn't very well apply for an executive position. Even with my many varied practical skills I couldn't expect to earn much more than three hundred a week. I was now faced with the reality of what I was up against and I didn't have much time to raise the cash. It was all so hopeless. I had no one to turn to. I no longer saw my friends because my partner didn't like them, and my parents had washed their hands of me shortly after becoming involved with him. They couldn't understand why I was allowing someone to control me and drag me down. The truth was I was shit scared of him and too proud to admit it. Maybe Peter's idea of going on the game wasn't so ridiculous.

Over the next couple of days I came to the realisation that unless I was prepared to lose my house I had no option. With my mind made up I drove to the local petrol station to pick up the free paper Peter had mentioned. I was shocked by the number of ladies advertising their services, some of which were blatantly obvious such as: *Busty Belinda offers relief.* The one thing most of them had in common was the mention of in/outcalls and no withheld numbers.

With that amount of competition I needed to think of something to make me stand out from the other ads. I wracked my brain for some time, and I don't know why but the name of a character in a famous kid's movie popped into my head: Truly Scrumptious. I then thought of different ads based around the name to keep it fresh, like: *Truly Scrumptious. Come and treat yourself,* or *Truly Scrumptious. Naughty but nice,* or *Truly Scrumptious. Indulge yourself.*

The next thing I needed to do was find out about prices. How could I do that? I couldn't very well phone these ladies to find out. I'd have to get a man to ring. Maybe Peter would help me out. As I hadn't yet told my partner what I was planning to do, I had to wait until he went out to buy cigarettes before I could phone Peter. He was very nice and said he'd make the calls and get back to me. After about fifteen minutes had passed, I started to think he wouldn't do it. *How stupid of me to involve a stranger*, I thought. I was feeling humiliated and disgusted, and nearly didn't answer the phone when it rang.

Peter gave me a list of services and prices that I jotted down: O with sixty, without eighty. Hand relief forty, massage and full personal ninety for half hour and one fifty for the hour. He laughed when I asked what O was, with or without, and what full personal meant. With some amusement he explained the various services in detail. He'd just finished when I told him I had to go as my partner had just got back from the shop.

Over the next couple of days I sorted out my wardrobe and underwear drawer. I made a firm decision that I would never do anything without a condom, no matter how much the guys were willing to pay. My next hurdle, before I could place the ad, was getting my partner to agree that I had no choice if I wanted to keep my house. I thought this would be my major problem, but it was impossible to do it behind his back, so I had to discuss it with him. I decided the best time to do this was on the way home after buying his puff, as he was always happy then. I'd have to withdraw what little money I had left in the post office, but I needed to butter him up. I couldn't believe how quickly he agreed to me doing it and he even told me his ex-wife had been a high-class escort when he'd met her. Any self-respecting woman would have questioned her relationship with a man who was allowing her to even consider going into prostitution. But my situation was so desperate that self-respect was simply a luxury I couldn't afford.

Chapter 3

The next morning I rang up and placed the ad. I was told the publication would be printed on Wednesday and be in the shops Thursday. As the day grew nearer I was becoming increasingly unsure about everything. When I spoke to my partner he said we had no choice and that if I did it he would do the same. That way we would get out of the shit quicker. I felt better knowing he was also prepared to sell himself.

On the Thursday morning, as I was making tea, the electric ran out so I had to boil a saucepan of water on the gas hob. I made breakfast for George and took it up to him. He wanted the day off school, claiming he had a headache. I wasn't having that and told him to hurry up or he'd be late.

When I returned from the school run my partner was up. He was in a foul mood, I guessed because we were out of electric so he couldn't go on the computer and chat to women online. Along with puff, this was his favourite pastime. We had even split up over it once! I decided to keep out of his way as much as possible and went upstairs to read. At 11 a.m. I realised I hadn't switched on my mobile that had the new SIM card. No sooner had I turned it on than it began to ring! I was totally unprepared and decided not to answer, and after several rings it stopped. Two minutes later it rang again and this time the caller was more persistent. I counted twenty rings.

It was at this point that my partner shouted up to me, 'There's no point in placing the ad if you're not going to answer the bloody phone!'

I didn't reply, but knew he was right. I would answer the next one.

'Hello, can I have details please?'

'Sorry, what do you mean?'

'I mean, what do you look like and how old are you?'

After giving him the information, he just said, 'Okay, can I get back to you a bit later?'

When I started to ask him what time that would be, he just put the phone down.

Throughout the day the calls kept coming. Most were like the first, but some were quite disgusting, asking things like: 'Are you shaved down below?' 'Do you have a big clit?' 'Can I eat you out?' One guy asked, 'How big are your tits?' and when I replied, he came back with, 'Can I wank off and rub my spunk all over them?'

'Certainly not! Bugger off, you dirty old sod!'

I put the phone down and started to laugh at myself for being such a prude. If I was to make money at this I was going to have to get used to dealing with all sorts. Another man rang and asked if I could dress as a schoolgirl and wee over him. When I said yes, he then asked if it could be done outside with him tied to a tree. And if that wasn't enough, he even wanted me to demand that he lick me clean. When I asked him if he would like me to come to his place, he replied, 'Oh no, you can't come to me, I'm married.'

It suddenly dawned on me what the in/outcalls meant.

I decided that the following week I would place the ad with outcalls only. That should put a stop to a lot of unnecessary calls from men wanting to visit me.

Henry got in early from college and shortly after I went and got George. I was not looking forward to telling him we didn't have electric. Like most kids he loved to sit himself in front of the TV when he got home from school.

Oh well, I thought, *sandwiches for dinner and an early night. Hopefully I might be able to borrow some money tomorrow.*

Just as I put the key in the door, my partner started. 'I've just about had enough of this. The fucking gas has just run out so we can't even cook dinner. What are you going to do about it?'

I really wanted to tell him to get off his arse and get a job, but knew if I did he would go crazy.

George quickly went up to his room and I followed him.

'Why don't you and Henry play a board game?'

'Okay, mum. What's for dinner? I'm starving.'

'I can make you some jam sandwiches, or cornflakes, if we have enough milk.'

'Can I have both?'

It was getting dark as I was making the sandwiches. I remembered I had some old Christmas candles in the cupboard under the stairs. I lit one and took it up on the tray with the food. George was in Henry's room and they were playing Monopoly.

'When's the electric going to be back on, mum?' asked Henry.

'I'm not sure yet. I'm going to try to borrow some money off someone later tonight. Be careful with the candle, boys.'

I went to my room and lay on the bed. The view from my window was beautiful, acres of green fields and massive oaks, with sheep scattered everywhere, looking like little blobs of golden fluff in the setting sun. I had always felt privileged to live in such an idyllic location, but for how much longer? I began to get a heavy, sinking feeling. As I lay there I told myself that crying wouldn't help. Action was needed if I was going to get out of this shit.

The phone was on my bedside cabinet. I had switched it off earlier when George got home. I reached for it and turned it on. I had voicemail but was out of credit so couldn't listen to it. I found myself willing the phone to ring. The wait was like sitting in the dentist's waiting room with toothache, knowing you need treatment desperately but not wanting it. Finally, the phone rang.

'Good evening, young lady. May I have an escort for tonight?'

'Yes, certainly. What time, and for how long?'

'For one hour, and as soon as possible, please. My address is . . .'

I interrupted at this point as I realised I didn't have a pen and paper. He must have thought I was very unprofessional. I rummaged in the bedside cabinet and thankfully found a pen.

'Sorry about that. What's your address?' I scribbled it inside the front cover of a novel I was reading. I could barely see with the failing light.

He then asked, 'What're the charges?'

'One fifty.'

'That's fine. How long do you think she will take to get here?'

'About an hour.'

'Okay, good. Thank you. By the way, do I pay the lady or by credit card now?'

'Just pay the lady.' I put the phone down and couldn't help laughing. The old gentleman obviously thought he was dealing with an escort agency. My first customer sounded okay. Maybe he would become a regular!

Chapter 4

I jumped off the bed and swung into action. The light was fading and I needed to apply make-up, so I ran downstairs and grabbed the other candle. My partner was sitting in the dining room with the dogs.

'I need you to come with me to Sevenoaks. A guy just rang. He wants a lady for an hour.'

'How much did you say?'

'One fifty.'

'Good. We can get some gas and electric, and I'm nearly out of cigarettes.'

It wasn't easy applying make-up by candlelight. I decided to wear a crutch-less black fishnet body stocking, as it hid a multitude of sins—I've had two 9Ib babies and have the stretch marks to prove it. The other worry was how to entertain a complete stranger for an hour. I certainly didn't want to shag him for that long. I'd just have to play it by ear.

I told the boys we were popping out and would be back with gas and electric. I reminded them to be careful with the candle and to put it out if they decided to go to bed.

When my partner started the car he said we only just had enough petrol. I then remembered I didn't have any condoms.

'Shit, we've no money for rubbers.'

'Well, that's it then. We may as well go back indoors.'

'Don't be stupid! Drive to the supermarket.'

'What're you going to do?'

'I'm going to steal them, of course.'

He parked the car in the darkest part of the car park, as though we were about to do an armed robbery. As I walked towards the entrance, I couldn't quite believe what I was about to do. Steal condoms at my age? What if I got caught? I imagined being caught by the security guard, marched to the office and the police being called. I didn't think I could go through with it, and then remembered my two boys sitting at home with a candle and not much to eat.

The display of condoms seemed endless: flavoured, coloured, ribbed, textured, ultrafine, and different brands and quantities. I spotted an Extra Safe box; that seemed the obvious choice. It was then that panicky thoughts entered my head. *What if I catch something? Or the rubber splits? Or comes off inside me?* I knew that was possible, as it had happened to me a few years earlier.

I was having a fling with a five-foot-four troll with a disturbing manic laugh. His idea of fucking was screwing me into the bed like he was boring for oil. I guess he thought he could give me a mind-blowing orgasm. What it did result in was a trip to A&E in the middle of the night, where a young doctor had to poke around with a pair of large forceps fishing for the lost condom. My embarrassment was made worse by the fact that the bloke responsible was sitting in the waiting room, warty faced, acne scarred and legs so short they dangled in midair as he sat on the chair. No matter how much I tried to convince myself that personality was the most important thing while lying on the table with my legs in stirrups, I decided Quasimodo the second had to go. The next weekend, after he damaged my Victorian iron and brass bed and couldn't care less, I told him to sling his hook.

I picked up a box of twelve extra safe condoms thinking that if I got caught it wasn't going to be for a pack of three. It was freezing cold and dark when I got outside the supermarket. The condoms were successfully stolen and concealed in my black fur coat that was also hiding what little I had on underneath.

I jumped in the car and said, 'Just drive.'

The house was a typical Victorian terraced cottage situated on a no-through road, with street parking only. We managed to find a space next door but one. As my partner manoeuvred the car I noticed the curtain move at the front window. The old gentleman looking to see if his escort had arrived, I supposed.

I looked at my partner and asked, 'Do you think I should do this?'

I wanted him to say he loved me too much to go through with it, but he merely replied, 'We don't have a choice. Anyway, we're here now, so you may as well take his money.'

I finally saw this man for what he was, and right then I hated him.

I got to the street door, and just as I was about to ring the bell it opened. The gentleman didn't look quite as old as I had imagined, probably about sixty-five. He looked a little unkempt, with balding straggly hair, a checked shirt and a brown bobble cardigan that wasn't done up properly, with two buttons dangling down onto his beige trousers.

'Come in, young lady. May I take your coat?'

As I slipped it off and handed it to him, I couldn't help noticing that he'd begun to shake slightly.

'What lovely big nipples you have. Can I suck them?'

'Yes, but you need to pay me first.'

'That's okay, my dear, I have the money all ready for you.'

He handed me a brown envelope that he had taken from his back pocket. I opened it and counted one hundred and fifty pounds. I placed the money back in the envelope and popped it in the pocket of my coat, now hanging on a coat stand in the hallway.

'Come on upstairs. I've put the electric fire on in the bedroom so it should be nice and warm.'

The room was drab and uninteresting with 1950s ugly brown furniture, a worn pink carpet and pink painted embossed walls. The bed had faded brown pillows and matching duvet. There was only one brown bedside cabinet on which sat a dirty ashtray, a box of tissues and a lamp with an orange pleated shade. I suggested that we turn the lamp on instead of the bare ceiling bulb, which he dutifully did before taking his clothes off and sitting on the edge of the bed.

'Come here, my lovely, and let me look at those tits.'

I did as I was told and stood close to him so I was between his legs. He began to fondle my breasts first with his fingers over the top of my body stocking, then he gently pulled the neckline down below my boobs and began to suck them. He grabbed hold of my buttocks and pulled me closer, at the same time moving his bottom nearer to the edge of the bed. I could feel his hard penis between my knees. It had begun to dribble and I knew it was time to put on the condom. I had placed a couple inside my high-heeled boots on the journey. I lifted one leg up and placed my foot on the bed, unzipping the boot and locating the condoms. I wanted to get on with the act and suggested he lay on the bed. As he lay down I slipped the condom on and got on top of him.

'Would you mind if I went on top? I prefer it that way.'

I told him yes, if he liked. I didn't really care, I just hoped he wouldn't take too long. As he mounted me I placed his dick inside and kept my fingers around it to prevent the condom from slipping off. As he pumped away I focused on the light bulb, from which cobwebs hung like garlands. The poor man obviously had no one in his life to care for him, that's why he needed my services.

After a few minutes he let out a groan and stopped thrusting. He rolled over onto his back and much to my relief the condom was intact, with the contents neatly contained. I got up from the bed and walked towards the door.

'Just a minute, dear, let me get dressed and I'll show you to the door.'

I watched him take off the condom and tissue himself clean. He wrapped the tissue and condom in a piece of newspaper, got dressed and walked me downstairs. I grabbed my coat from the stand and checked the pocket as I put it on. Going towards the door, he grabbed my hand and placed a screwed-up note in it.

'That's for you, dear, not the agency. Thank you and goodnight.'

As I walked out of the house my partner started the engine and drove past me. For a split second I panicked and then realised he was just turning the car around.

'Well, how'd it go?'

'He was okay, no trouble.'

'Did he pay you?'

'Yes, of course.'

I still had the screwed-up note in my hand but didn't tell him. I'd earned that tip and wasn't going to share it with him. I told him if we hurried up we'd make it to the late-night supermarket; I was starving. The wonderful feeling of walking around the store and filling the trolley soon took away any doubts about what I had just done. My partner said we deserved a bottle of wine and I thought *We?*

He pulled into the petrol station and put in twenty pounds worth. Thankfully, he'd remembered the gas and electric cards so we could top them up there. It made me think of the boys back at home. I was sure they were fine. Henry was a mature seventeen year old and quite capable of looking after his younger brother. Nevertheless, I wanted to get home as soon as possible.

It was about 11 o'clock when we got back home. The candle had been extinguished and the boys were sound asleep. I didn't see any point in waking them and quietly closed their doors. When I went downstairs, my partner, after switching the electric back on, was already sitting in front of the computer. I decided to make a tea and go up to bed, even though I felt wide awake. I guess I was still buzzing from the evening.

My partner came up to bed soon after me. I thought that was a bit strange as he would normally be on the computer (chatting to strangers that I called 'sad chat room fucks' when I was angry) until the early hours of the morning. Then he did another thing out of character. He cuddled and caressed me, then gently fingered my fanny. I became very aroused after a few minutes and he was rock hard. I was very wet and didn't have to guide him in. His technique was usually hard and rough, but this time he was slow and tender. I thought he was trying to reassure me that what I'd done was okay and he still loved me.

Chapter 5

Islept well considering what I had done the previous evening and was woken by the alarm clock. I woke the boys, and they both immediately switched their TVs on when I told them we had electric.

'Come on, you haven't got time to watch telly. You'll be late. Hurry up and get dressed while I do breakfast.'

'But George drank the rest of the milk while you were out last night.'

'Don't worry, there's milk and food.'

'Brilliant!' exclaimed George.

'Where'd you get the money from?' asked Henry.

'I borrowed it from a friend. Now hurry up and get ready or you'll not have time for breakfast.'

As I had enough petrol I dropped Henry off at college after taking George to school. It was 10 a.m. when I got back home and turned the work phone on. I'd received more voicemails and a few text messages asking me to get back with details. There were also a few disgusting ones that I deleted. I decided, then and there, that I wasn't going to tolerate abusive or bad mannered men. I was living with one and that was enough.

Over the following weeks I took hundreds of calls, mainly from guys wanting to visit me, even though I'd reworded my original ad. I was beginning to realise there wasn't enough work for outcalls only. On average, I visited three men a week. I knew by then that if I wanted to make money I needed a place to work from. In the meantime, I decided to reinvent myself. But how?

I pondered over the ads in the paper. Apart from a transvestite and a dominatrix offering telephone sex, all the ads were similar. It was while watching a Carry On film one afternoon that I thought of doing a naughty nurse. I didn't even have to buy a uniform, as an old boyfriend who liked me to dress up kinky had bought me an original.

I bought another phone so the nurse would have a different number from Truly Scrumptious. The ad read *Nurse Naughty on duty for treatment and relief—visiting service by appointment.* After placing the ad, I waited anxiously for the response. I received calls from men wanting all kinds of treatment from sex to prostate check-ups. Some of them must have thought I was a real nurse.

The evening the nurse ad came out I took a call from a very well-spoken old gentleman who said he desperately needed my help, and asked if I'd come out and administer the appropriate treatment. I told him my fees and we agreed on a time. My partner was happy when I told him I had a job not far from us, about five miles way. He'd started getting fed up of accompanying me to jobs and even accused me of being a workaholic. This pissed me off, as he was quite happy spending the money I'd earned. After quite a bit of persuading and the promise of some puff, he drove me to the job.

The old gent had switched on the porch light for me. I thought that was very sweet, as most punters were reluctant to do so for fear of their neighbours seeing me. I often had to reassure them over the phone that I was very discreet and would not go to their door dressed in anything obvious.

The door opened and at first I was unable to see my client, as he was tucked behind the street door. It was only after he ushered me in and closed the door that I realised why he was hiding.

'Thank you, nurse, for coming to see me. I just can't help myself. I have this terrible urge to go out like this, but what would people say?'

I thought for a moment before replying, 'It's a bit cold outside to be wearing only a negligee and sandals. I think you need advice on appropriate clothing if you want to go out in the future.'

Much to my relief he appeared delighted with this suggestion and showed me into his sitting room. He insisted on making tea and biscuits for us both, which he brought in on a tray along with my consultation fee.

He then opened up to me. John was secretly Janine and had been hiding this for over fifty years. Apparently, I was the first person he'd told, apart from his wife, who had recently died. She found out after being married to him for over thirty years when she'd come home early from shopping one Saturday afternoon. She usually had her hair done every month, regular as clockwork, but this particular day she had a headache. She walked in and found him dressed as Janine. He was wearing her best red satin dress and stockings, and had even attempted to squeeze into a pair of her court shoes. Needless to say, she went bats and made him burn the items of clothing. They never spoke about the incident again.

I felt sorry for him and offered to go shopping on his behalf for some larger items of ladies clothing. He was so overwhelmed with emotion that he cried. I think it was because he'd just offloaded a secret he'd held onto for far too long.

Nurse Naughty proved so popular she was getting more calls than the ad for Truly Scrumptious, which was mainly attracting punters wanting a cheap sexual service. I kept the two ads running as I needed the money, even though I hated having sex with punters. It was also causing problems in my relationship, as my partner was becoming more and more resentful of what I was doing. Whenever we argued, he'd say things like, 'How can you sell yourself? I couldn't do that, no matter how desperate.' He didn't have to when he had me doing it. He was no better than a pimp!

I was in the middle of cooking dinner one evening when the phone rang. The boys were upstairs playing a computer game very loudly, so I knew they were unable to hear. I'd managed to be discreet so far and wanted it to stay that way. I could hardly understand what the old man was saying at first. I thought he must have had a stroke because his speech was very slurred, but he didn't sound drunk. I'd taken plenty of calls from drunks, so I knew he wasn't one of them. I told him to take his time and speak slowly.

'Can I have a lady for this evening?'

'Yes, darling, but it will be one hundred and fifty pounds.'

'Can she wear a short skirt? And tell her I like to kiss and cuddle.'

I asked for his address and after giving it he asked, 'What time can she get here?'

'She'll be a couple of hours.'

'Don't forget to tell her to wear a short skirt.'

After dinner I went upstairs to get ready. I felt sorry for the old chap and wanted to look my best for him. I put on a black bra and matching knickers, lacy-topped black stockings and suspender belt, and a pair of high-heeled stilettos. I looked in the back of the wardrobe and found a little black Karen Millen skirt and matching camisole top. It was years old and I hadn't worn it for ages, as I felt too old to wear short skirts. But if that's what the punter wanted, that's what he'd get. After all, he was paying.

It was a half-hour drive to the punter's house and my partner was silent for most of it, only opening his mouth to swear at another driver and to mention he was out of puff. I knew that meant a late-night drug run after I'd done the job. We arrived at a council estate, and after driving around for quite some time and asking for directions we eventually found the road—a row of little 1970s council houses. I told my partner the house number was forty-five and he parked a few doors down.

I knocked on the door, but got no reply. The house was in total darkness. I knocked again and after a few seconds went back to the car. The guy was obviously a time-waster. Just as I crossed the road, walking towards the car, the door of number forty-four opened and a little old man walked to the front gate.

'Are you my escort?' he shouted.

I was so panic-stricken in case the neighbours called the police that I ignored him and rushed to the car, thinking, *Why does he have to park so far away?*

The punter then shouted, 'You are my escort. You're wearing a short skirt.'

I opened the door and dived in the car. My partner asked what all the shouting was about and I told him to just drive me home. On the way, when I explained what had happened, he blamed me for writing down the wrong address.

The next morning, after switching the phone on, the old man rang asking what had happened to his escort. I pretended I didn't know and apologised. He sounded so upset I promised to send him out another girl for that night. I put the phone down and decided to dress as Nurse Naughty, so he wouldn't recognise me with my hair tied up and glasses on. My uniform dress was very short, so he'd be pleased.

That night we set off again and arrived, as planned, a little early. I quietly opened the gate and walked up the path. I undid my coat to reveal my short dress and rang the bell. After a few moments the porch light came on and I could see someone through the half glass door. When it opened the stench of piss nearly knocked me out. A little old man on a walking frame stood before me; his face dropped on one side and he was dribbling.

He'd obviously had a stroke. He asked me in and I hesitated for a moment, thinking, *do I really want to do a pissy old man?* But I'd let him down once so I couldn't possibly do it a second time.

I took off my coat and stood for a second before asking, 'Would you care to pay me first, love?'

'What do you mean, pay you?'

'The lady on the phone must have told you the rates are one hundred and fifty pounds.'

'But you're the nurse!' he exclaimed. 'I don't pay for the nurse, she's on the NHS, she's free.'

I put my coat back on and left, thinking *let that be a lesson.* It didn't feel right the night before, and I should have trusted my instincts and not gone back a second time. I certainly shouldn't feel sorry for punters. This was just a job.

A few days later I saw the funny side and laughed about it, thinking he couldn't get my kind of treatment on the NHS.

Chapter 6

I'd started having the occasional punter come to my house when the boys were at school and college. They were strictly by appointment and with those I'd already visited at their homes. This had been my partner's suggestion so we could earn more money and get some premises. It worked okay. The neighbours didn't seem to notice, and I insisted the men came smartly dressed as if they were on business. My partner stayed in the dining room out of the way while I entertained. I'd also started advertising on the Internet. The men would read my profile and email me if they were interested.

My partner decided it was his job to read them and reply if he thought they were suitable. If the guy wanted to give or receive, have oral without or anal sex, he wasn't given the mobile number. I was quite happy to let him do this job, as I wasn't very good on the computer and didn't really have the time.

I was constantly trying to think of ways to make more money. I had recently confided in my friend, Beulah, who was also in financial difficulty. Her problems were a lot worse than mine and she was desperate for money. She suggested we work together, offering punters a double act. I didn't see what harm it could do and agreed. I mentioned the idea to my partner and he was okay about it, so I placed an ad for the Dynamic Duo. Needless to say, the phone rang as soon as the ad came out and we received a booking that night for three hundred and sixty pounds.

My partner was happy when I told him he didn't need to come as I felt Beulah and I would be safe together. I picked her up at home as she didn't have a car and we drove to a place called Hildenborough. I knew the area vaguely as I'd nearly bought a house there a few years before. Beulah chatted constantly on the journey about what we should do to the guy and how we should avoid sex with him. I was beginning to have my doubts about her and suggested she may not be up for the job.

'You worry too much,' she said. 'You seem to forget I'm a fully qualified aromatherapy masseuse. I'm used to dealing with men.'

I decided to shut up and just wait to see how she performed. She'd brought a large sports bag with her, telling me it contained towels, aromatherapy oils and two beautician dresses.

'Beulah, we have everything we need: condoms, baby wipes and a couple of pairs of tits and fannies.'

She laughed and said, 'Okay, I get your point, but let's at least wear the dresses. They're sexy, and men seem to like them.'

We pulled into a lay-by, took off our jeans and jumpers, and put the dresses on. I must admit she was right, they did look sexy, especially with sheer stockings and high heels. We continued our journey, and when we arrived I parked up at the corner of the little cul-de-sac. We both reapplied our lipstick before taking a deep breath and getting out of the car. For some reason I was more nervous than usual, I think because I could sense Beulah's fear.

I rang the doorbell and what sounded like a pack of wolves started jumping up at the door. I heard a man shout, 'Get in here, dogs.' After a second or two, the door opened. A tall man, about sixty years old with an Elvis-style haircut complete with sideburns, asked us in.

We stood in the hallway while he blatantly looked us up and down, and then said, 'You'll do, girls.'

I asked for the money and he said it was in the lounge. We followed him down a rather long corridor, and as we were about to pass a stable door, its lower half closed, two huge hairy German Shepherds jumped up. Beulah was inches away when this happened, and she screamed and fell back on me.

The punter laughed and said, 'Don't worry, ladies, they won't hurt you. They can't get over the door.'

'Are you sure?' I asked.

'Yeah, quite sure, as long as I'm happy with what I get.'

We were shown into the lounge. It was jam-packed with furniture: two big cream leather sofas with frilly piping and a matching recliner, green shagpile carpet and a dark wooden sideboard with glass sliding doors and crystal glasses inside. The top was full of bottles of drink, and in one corner of the room was a large flat-screen telly. There was also a quality music system playing 'Are You Lonesome Tonight?'

'Okay, girls, I'm just going to the loo. Make yourselves comfy, I won't be a minute.'

'Come on, let's get ready, I want to get out of here as soon as possible,' Beulah said when he'd gone.

'But, Beulah, we have to give him his time for the kind of money we're charging or he'll get pissed off, and don't forget the dogs.'

'He wouldn't set them on us, would he?'

'I doubt it, but you never know with punters. Shush, I can hear him coming back.'

He walked in stark naked! I caught a glimpse of Beulah's surprised look and grinned at her. Nothing shocked me any more. I'd seen all shapes and sizes and this guy was averagely built in every way.

I suggested we go up to his bedroom, but he said he was happier in the lounge because of the music system. He then walked over to the sideboard and took a wad of notes from the drawer. He clearly thought I was the boss as he handed it to me. I counted the money in front of him and put it in my dress pocket.

'Where do you want me, ladies?'

'Lying on your tummy, on the floor,' suggested Beulah. She took a large white towel out of her bag and a bottle of massage oil. The guy did as asked and lay on the towel. I grabbed a pillow from the couch and placed it under his head. Beulah then straddled him, poured some oil on her hands and started working on his neck and shoulders. I couldn't believe it, she was actually giving him a professional massage. After several minutes of observing this I realised I'd have to take the initiative, as she obviously had no intention of doing anything sexual to this man. I mouthed to her to get off him.

'Would you like to roll over onto your back please, darling?'

'I was beginning to wonder when you were going to start sorting me out.'

His dick was soft; obviously the massage wasn't doing a thing. I suspected this guy was a seasoned punter who'd had more than his fair share of working girls and wasn't easily turned on. Beulah was now massaging his legs, making sure to avoid the most important area.

I thought, *Fuck, if I don't do something fast he's going to want his money back, and who could blame him?* I stripped off my dress and stood over his face. I had on my trusty crutchless black body stocking. I lowered myself down so that I was squatting with my fanny touching his lips. I was facing Beulah, who was watching in disbelief. I mouthed to her to get her tits out and she shook her head and mouthed back *no way*. I realised it was up to me to pull this off. I blocked Beulah out of my mind and took control.

'Lick me!' I commanded. He didn't hesitate, going straight in. I let him do this for a while and then stood up.

'Please, let me do more?'

'No, shut up, I'm in charge! Now put your hands behind your head and keep them there.'

He seemed to enjoy being spoken to sternly as I noticed his cock was starting to get hard. I asked Beulah to pass me a condom and it went on easily as he was now rock hard. I stood over him and lowered myself down, slowly, like before, but this time over his cock. I guided him in and at that moment he removed his hands.

'Put your hands back behind your head and keep them there until I tell you otherwise!'

'Okay, bitch.'

I knew not to be worried as he was just getting into the role. I went up and down very slowly a few times, then got off him.

'What are you doing? I was enjoying that.'

'Shut up and stay there!'

As he lay with his dick throbbing, I walked over to the sports bag and took out the Mars bar we'd bought earlier at the petrol station. I sat on the sofa that would give him the best view, spread my legs open and slowly took off the wrapper. Then I spread my labs open with two fingers and inserted the chocolate bar.

'Now remove your hands and start wanking!'

I worked the Mars bar in and out several times, and as the chocolate melted and dribbled everywhere he came. Beulah was massaging his legs again at the time and some of his sperm went in her hair. I'll never forget the look of utter disgust on her face—what a picture!

I wrapped the Mars bar in tissue and got dressed, while Beulah rolled the towel up and put it in the bag. The punter disappeared and came back wearing a white towel robe. He thanked us for giving him such a good time, especially the show with the Mars bar—he'd never seen that done before.

As we walked the short distance back to the car, Beulah said, 'I can't believe you did that with the Mars bar. Why didn't you let me massage him till he came?'

'Don't be ridiculous, Beulah, we'd have been there all night. Couldn't you see he wasn't getting hard?'

'I just needed to work on him a bit longer.'

'Maybe if you'd got your tits out it would have helped.'

'I wasn't going to do that for that dirty old man.'

'But you must have known what the job entails?'

'Okay, okay, I'll get it right next time. Anyway, let's go and have a drink. I could do with one.'

We parked in the lay-by again and changed back into our clothes before driving on to the village pub, where I ordered two gin and tonics and a couple of bags of crisps.

The barman looked at us and asked, 'Hard night, girls?'

Beulah and I looked at each other, wondering how much he knew. We made no comment, and it was only when we went to the brightly lit toilet and looked in the mirror we understood. We both looked a bloody mess, with mascara running and scruffy hair. If only the barman knew what we'd been up to; that would give the locals something to talk about.

On the way back to Beulah's we chatted about what she was prepared to do the next time. As I suspected, the list of don'ts far outweighed the dos. She even suggested I do the sex and she'd do the massage, but still split the money fifty-fifty. I said I thought that was a bit unfair but would think about it. When we arrived at her place she said it was best if I didn't come in, as her husband wasn't aware what kind of massage we were offering and he might ask some awkward questions. That was fine by me, I was tired and just wanted to get home. I counted out one hundred and eighty pounds and she gave me ten back for petrol.

Chapter 7

On the way back home, I decided that if Beulah wasn't prepared to give guys sex then she wasn't cut out for the job. She certainly couldn't expect me to do all the work and have half of the money. I may as well work for a madam! When I got home, my partner wanted to know all about the evening. When I told him what had happened, he said, 'Why did you give her half the money when it was you who sorted the guy out?'

'I'd already agreed to.'

'So what? The guy gave you the money, not her. You should have given her a hundred tops.'

'You're right. When she rings tomorrow, I'll have a word.'

The rest of the evening was quite pleasant because my partner was in a good mood for a change. This was probably because he had a nice lump of puff we'd bought the day before, and the boys were visiting their father for the weekend. We sat and drank wine and ate the pizza I'd bought on the way home. I suggested we take the rest of the wine up to bed and watch telly. Much to my surprise, he agreed.

'But I need to check my emails first,' he said.

I told myself not to get angry, as it would spoil the evening. So while he was on the computer, I took the dogs for a walk.

The next morning I received a call.

'Good morning, nurse, it's Peter. Do you recall I spoke to you last weekend about having anal treatment and you told me to ring back on the day I required the visit?'

'Oh yes, Peter, I remember.'

'Well, my wife has gone to a horse show and won't be back till 3 o'clock, so is it possible to visit me this morning?'

'Yes, Peter, what's your address?'

After I had written it down, he asked, 'How soon can you get here?'

'About an hour, is that okay?'

'Yes, that's fine. See you soon, nurse.'

When I'd finished talking to him, I began to remember the conversation I'd had with him the week before when he'd asked a lot of questions. It was because of this that I thought he was a wank off. I gave this title for the obvious reason. They were men that rang working girls' numbers so they could have a cheap wank instead of using 0909 premium numbers. Experience had taught me to now listen to the slightest change in the voices to detect a wanker.

I didn't have enough time to shower and wash my hair, so I just stood in the bath and washed the important bits. I was sure this punter wasn't going to be fussed about my personal hygiene as I was only going to examine his bottom. I knew fucking was out of the question because he told me he couldn't get an erection due to the medication he was taking. I grabbed a pair of tights from the drawer and noticed a hole. They'd have to do; I didn't have any stockings because I'd binned them all and forgotten to replace them when I went to the supermarket. I slapped on my make-up and put on the nurse's uniform, with jeans and jumper over the top. I told my partner I had a job and would be back in a couple of hours. I didn't hassle him to come with me as it was daytime and I felt I'd be safe.

When I arrived at the punter's house, I couldn't help feeling jealous. It was gorgeous, just like the kind on the front of chocolate boxes, set in its own extensive grounds down a quiet country lane. I couldn't wait to go inside and have a look around. As soon as I parked the car on the driveway the gent came out to greet me.

'Good morning, my dear. Thank you for coming.'

'What a beautiful house you have. I can't wait to go in.'

He grinned at me and said, 'I, too, can't wait to go in.'

I ignored his obvious suggestive remark, took my briefcase from the boot of the car and followed him into a large sitting room with a huge inglenook fireplace and oak-beamed ceiling. Persian rugs were scattered over the wooden floor and the furniture was an assortment of comfy chairs and sofas. Nothing matched, but it went beautifully together. After admiring the room for a few moments, I was led along a small corridor and then up a rather narrow flight of creaky stairs and into a beautiful bedroom. This also had beams and polished wooden floorboards.

I noticed my fees had been placed on the bedside cabinet, and just as I was going to ask for the money, Peter handed it to me.

'I think you'll find this is the correct amount. You did say one hundred and fifty?'

'Yes, that's right, I did.' I counted the money as I always did after being short-changed once. I'm not sure if that had been a genuine mistake, but it taught me not to trust any of them. Sometimes punters pay too much, probably from nerves or excitement, and after counting the money I smile sweetly and say, 'That's correct, darling.' I never feel guilty, as I consider it a tip in advance of my services.

'Now, Peter, shall we play nurse and patient?'

He looked at me for a second or two and said, 'I would rather play doctor and patient.'

'Okay, I can be a doctor if you prefer that.'

'No, not you, me. I want to examine your bottom with my finger.'

I hesitated for a moment before replying that I didn't usually allow punters to do anal play, but as he was only going to insert a finger I didn't see the harm.

'I don't mind as long as you wear a pair of my disposable gloves.'

He agreed to wear them and then the session began. I bent over the bed and he inserted his finger. Even though he was wearing gloves I could still feel his fingernail scratching my internal piles. After about fifteen minutes of this, I decided he'd have to stop because my bottom was getting very sore, but it was too early to finish the session so I needed to distract him.

'Doctor, I need you to examine my breasts. Shall I lie down on the bed so you can have a good feel of them?'

He eagerly agreed and thankfully removed his finger from my arse, which was now burning with pain. I'd suffered on and off with haemorrhoids for years and I can honestly say anal play was far from a pleasant experience. Peter began to wank his flaccid little dick while rubbing it against my nipples. I knew from experience that punters didn't need to get hard to come. It would just take longer for him to climax, especially because he was on medication. I assisted him by squeezing my tits together so he had a bit more feeling, and moaned as if I was having an orgasm. Eventually, he came. *Thank goodness for that*, I thought. He was really beginning to be a pain in the arse, in more ways than one.

When I got back to the car and checked my phone, I realised I had another pain to deal with—Beulah. She'd called four times. I knew I'd have to deal with her soon as she was a very persistent person who didn't take no for an answer. But it was Saturday and I was looking forward to having the weekend off.

Chapter 8

Over the weekend I received a call from a young woman who was looking for work. She said she'd been working in a massage parlour in Brighton a couple of days a week, but wanted to find somewhere a bit closer. I asked if she minded doing outcalls and would be happy doing a double act. I arranged to meet her on Monday at a café in Tunbridge Wells so we could have a good chat. I was looking forward to meeting someone with experience at working in a brothel. When I told my partner about the call and the arranged meeting, he said it would be better working with an experienced girl than Beulah.

I walked into the café that Monday, and sitting in the corner was a young woman matching the description. She had long reddish-brown hair, was a little overweight, with large boobs and a very pretty face. I knew the extra few pounds in weight would not be a problem because most punters seemed to prefer it. I decided to introduce myself using my work name; I thought until I got to know her the less she knew the better.

I walked up to her and said, 'Hi, you must be Gemma, my name's Truly.

'It's lovely to meet you, Truly.'

We ordered coffee and sat chatting like we'd known each other for years. She told me the rates she was on in Brighton and I agreed to pay her the same. I'd expected her to ask for more.

I took her mobile number and said I'd call when I received a booking. It didn't take long before a call came in from a guy wanting a double act that evening at 8 p.m. I rang Gemma and arranged to meet her at his address, and she told me she drove a green Rover. When I arrived, at exactly 8 o'clock, she was already there. *That's a good start*, I thought.

As we walked to the door I quickly filled Gemma in on what the punter wanted and she replied in a matter-of-fact tone, 'Oh, that's straightforward stuff. He just wants a little show from us, as if we are lesbian lovers. We can suck one another's tits and finger each other. That should be enough to get him going. Are you okay with that, Truly?'

'Yeah, why not? You are obviously more experienced, I'll just leave it up to you.'

The session went really well. The punter was so excited watching us sucking tits and fingering each other; we even pretended to lick one another. After a while the guy couldn't take any more and he began to wank.

Just as Gemma asked, 'Do you want to fuck?' he let out a loud groan and shot his load, exclaiming, 'That was fucking fantastic! I've never seen two girls at it before.'

We took our clothes into the bathroom and washed and tidied ourselves.

Gemma looked at me and smiled. 'That was easy, wasn't it, Truly?'

'Yes, it was, thanks to you.'

Gemma sat in my car while I counted out her share of the money. My private mobile rang and I recognised Beulah's number.

'Would you do me a favour, Gemma? Answer this and say I'm busy. I don't want to talk to this person right now.'

She answered without hesitating. 'Hello, Truly can't get to the phone at the moment, she's in the bathroom.'

I could hear Beulah shout, 'Who are you, and why are you answering her phone?'

Gemma remained perfectly calm and politely replied, 'I'm a friend. Do you want me to get her to call you back?' She handed the phone back saying, 'The stroppy bitch has hung up.'

I would have to ring Beulah back and be honest with her. I didn't know why I was feeling guilty; she hadn't invested any money and didn't want to have sex with punters. Not that I could blame her for that, but she wasn't my responsibility, and I wasn't in a position to carry someone.

Not long after getting back from the school run the next morning while having breakfast with my partner, Beulah rang. I calmly explained that unless she was prepared to offer sexual services there was no point in us working together. She then accused me of going behind her back.

My partner grabbed the phone and said, 'If you're prepared to open your legs, fine. If not, how can you possibly expect to take half the money?'

I'm not sure what she said next, because he put the phone down on her.

He smiled and said, 'That's the last we'll hear from that stupid bitch.'

I made no comment, but deep down I was very worried. Beulah once told me she always got her revenge when someone wronged her. She told me she went to kill her ex-husband with a stun gun, but the police arrested her outside his house. I told myself she was probably lying and that it was just a fantasy about what she'd like to do to him. Nevertheless, I went to bed that night feeling very uneasy about having made an enemy of her.

Over the next few days, Gemma and I visited several clients. Working together made the work so much more fun. She often made me laugh by pulling silly faces when the guy was fucking her. He never noticed because she favoured the doggy position, and he was too busy looking at her arse and what I was doing. She also taught me how to answer the phone so as to keep within the law as much as possible: don't be explicit about the services on offer, don't tell the punter what you do but wait for him to tell you what he wants, don't mention pounds, just say one fifty for example when he asks how much, don't give any information to punters that withhold their numbers, never give your address until they've arrived in the area for their appointment and always take a landline number for an outcall and ring back to check it's him. I listened in earnest to what she was saying and took her advice—after all, she was far more experienced than I.

Gemma wasn't going to be available to work over the weekend and therefore I decided to have a break from the punters.

Chapter 9

I was in the shower when I heard the doorbell ring. My partner shouted, 'I'll get it!'

I got out of the shower and listened through the crack in the door. I recognised the voice of my neighbour, Graham, from the house opposite. *What does he want?* I wondered as I grabbed my robe and went downstairs. My partner was reading a sheet of paper.

'What's that, more junk mail?' I asked.

Graham looked at me and said, 'I think you need to read this. It was put through my door late last night.'

I took the piece of paper and read.

NEIGHBOURHOOD WATCH NOTICE

Are you aware that 45 Meadow Road is operating as a brothel? The madam receives up to twenty visitors a day. Her partner downloads and watches pornography. Please be careful of your teenage daughters, this man may try to recruit them. If you do not believe this notice, ring this number and you'll find it's true. If you look in the free paper you'll find the same number.

Graham then said, 'I tried ringing the number this morning, but it's switched off. Anyway, I know this can't be true. It's obviously someone's idea of a sick joke. You should pop round to the man who's the head of neighbourhood watch. He rang the police last night when the letter was put through his door because he didn't want people to think it an official notice.'

'What are we going to do?' I asked.

'I think we should go to the police.'

'Are you mad?'

'No. We have nothing to worry about, they have no proof. Now hurry up and get dressed so we can go to the police station.'

On the way we talked about who could have done this to us, but there was really only one possibility—Beulah. I began to think maybe she really did try to kill her husband. Then I remembered another conversation we'd had some time ago. I must admit we were drunk, but it was still a bit disconcerting. She wanted to have another go at killing her ex-husband and asked if she hired a van would I drive it. The plan was to drive to his house with her and the new husband hiding in the back. When he came out of the house and walked by, they'd open the back doors, pull him in, smash a brick over his head, then drive somewhere and dump the body. I just laughed at the crazy idea and told her she was drunk.

I was now starting to panic. What if she tried to kill one of us, or the boys? I'd read about crazy people in the newspapers, but never thought I'd come across one. Feelings of guilt flooded in. I should never have told Beulah what I was doing and never entertained anyone at home, no matter how much we needed the money. If I was going to continue this work I needed to find premises.

The police took a copy of the letter and said they'd send an officer to our home as they were extremely busy at the station. That evening, at seven, two officers arrived. The boys had gone to the cinema so we were free to talk. We were asked if we had any idea who'd done this. I gave them Beulah and her husband's names and address. One of the officers asked why I thought it was them, and I told him I'd recently fallen out with Beulah over a business matter.

He looked at the letter and asked, 'Is this your mobile number?'

'Yes, it is.'

'And are you advertising in the free paper?'

'Yes, I do aromatherapy massage.' I must have looked worried, because the officer then said, 'It's no problem, miss, you're not in any trouble. It's just that we take this problem very seriously and want to protect you and your family.'

'What do you mean?' asked my partner.

'Well, this kind of thing can upset people in the neighbourhood, and some silly people try to take the law into their own hands.'

'Do you think anyone would believe this letter?' asked my partner.

'It's possible,' one of the officers replied.

'So what will happen now?' I asked.

'We'll have a word with them and get back to you. Is that okay?'

'Yes, thanks, officers.'

As I showed them to the door, one of them said, 'If you have any problems, don't hesitate to dial 999. Take care, and goodnight.'

After the police left, it was time to collect the boys from the cinema. On the way, we decided it was best to keep the matter from them. Fortunately, they didn't attend local schools and so hopefully the other kids didn't know about the letter. When the boys went to bed we stayed up talking about the situation. I hadn't switched the phone on, and my partner suggested destroying the SIM card and not advertising for a while until things settled down. I'd also have to let Gemma know what was going on. Fortunately, I'd earned a fair amount of money recently and hidden some in a Cornflakes box for emergencies. I lay in bed that night wondering how the neighbours would treat us; surely they wouldn't believe the letter, I'd been far too discreet.

I found out the next morning. When I put the rubbish out in the shared driveway, my neighbour, Janine, was putting hers out at the same time. Normally she was very chatty, but that morning she totally ignored me and quickly went back indoors. The same thing happened to my partner that afternoon when he was washing the car. Her two young children were playing in the driveway and he talked to them as usual. Janine suddenly appeared and screamed at the kids to get inside for no apparent reason. Her voice was nearly hysterical, as though they were facing imminent danger.

Later that evening as we walked the dogs, people crossed the road to avoid us and a couple of teenagers shouted, 'Madam and Pimp.' We just ignored them and quickened our pace.

'I wonder how many letters they delivered?' I asked him.

'It doesn't matter. This is a small town and news travels fast.'

'I think we need to move.'

He agreed, and later that evening we made the decision to get the house ready to sell. It needed a new kitchen and bathroom, plus redecorating throughout. This meant I was going to have to work even harder.

Just when I thought things couldn't get any worse, they did. The next morning, a gentleman from Social Services knocked and said he'd received an anonymous call from a person who suspected a child was being abused. I told him about the letter and that the police were investigating the matter. I gave him the police officer's name so he could confirm it was true. He asked for the names of everyone living in the house, gave me his card and said he'd call again after making the necessary enquiries.

As soon as he'd gone I phoned my solicitor, Andrew, whom I'd met the year before while attending the police station on a matter regarding my son, Henry. Since then, he'd become a very dear friend and confidant. He was so supportive and understanding, and offered to help in anyway he could, be it professional or personal.

A couple of hours later I opened the door to an RSPCA gentleman asking if he could come in and have a chat.

By now I was beginning to see how funny and ridiculous everything was becoming, and trying not to laugh I said, 'Come in, everyone else has!'

He looked at me strangely as I showed him through to the dining room, from where he could see the dogs playing happily in the garden.

'I'm sorry, miss, but I've just received a report regarding your dogs. Apparently, they're allowed to run around the streets, are aggressive and are badly treated.'

'Let me show you the dogs.' I called them in and one of them ran straight up to him and started licking his hand.

'She's only a baby,' he said as the other dog bounded over to me.

'And he's a mummy's boy and not the slightest bit interested in strangers.'

'He's beautiful. Have you had him long?'

'I've had him from twelve weeks old, and he's seven now. I can assure you he's spoilt rotten, and the dogs are never allowed to wander the streets alone.'

'Don't worry, lady, I can see they're both well looked after. This was obviously a hoax call—we get a fair few you know.'

'I'm sure you do.'

'I'm sorry to have wasted your time, miss.'

'It's okay, I understand you have to take every call seriously.'

When he left, I poured a large gin and tonic, and after calming down told myself Beulah wasn't going to break me. My partner couldn't cope with the stress of it all and left me to deal with everything. His way of coping with things was to shut himself away and smoke more weed.

A couple of days passed before we heard from the police. An officer rang to ask if we'd be home so he could give us an update. Soon after the call he arrived with some great news: Beulah and her husband had been seen by the police posting letters and were told to stop and go home. They were spotted later still posting letters and this time were arrested and put in the cells after becoming very violent towards the police.

'We're going to fit your house with a panic alarm that's linked directly to the police station.'

'Why do we need one? It sounds a bit extreme.'

'It's just a precaution in case Beulah and her husband decide to come round. It appears they tried to harm someone before, so we don't want to take any chances.'

I agreed to the alarm being fitted and about an hour later the guy came round and installed it.

When I rang Andrew later that day and told him about it, he laughed and said, 'You must be the only working lady that has a panic alarm linked directly to the police station.'

A few days later, the police came round and told us that Beulah and her husband were not allowed within a four-mile radius of our house and, if caught in the area, would be immediately arrested. I slept soundly that night knowing the police had taken the matter seriously. I would start working again in another week or so. By then things should have quietened down.

Chapter 10

I made the decision to no longer offer sexual services at home but become a dominatrix instead. I'd been looking on the Internet and realised there was a demand for it, but if I were to charge high prices I'd need a dungeon and equipment. With that set-up I'd only need to see one or two gentlemen a day to earn good money. I made a list of items I had around the house that would be useful: a school desk and easel, a saw bench that could be padded and upholstered to use as a whipping bench, a large dog cage and riding crop, handcuffs and high-heeled stiletto boots.

I took a trip to the sex shop and bought a selection of butt plugs, whips and paddles, a black rubber dress, a pair of door restraints, a studded dog collar and a lead.

I took the items to the counter and the lady working there asked, 'Are you just starting up?' When I confirmed, she said, 'Well, you should think about buying the Electric Stim equipment, guys like it.'

'What the hell's that? I've never heard of it.'

She took me over to a glass display cabinet and took a couple of black boxes out.

'This is a battery Stim kit and you can buy various different attachments such as these electric pinchers. You use them to pinch their penis and balls, which then sends an electric current, and this attachment is a pinwheel.'

'It looks like a pastry cutter.'

'Yes, but you don't cut with it, you just lightly pass it over their genitals. The electric current makes them feel like they're being cut with a hot knife. It's one of the most popular attachments. Or what about this metal probe? It's straightforward . . . just stick it up their arse.'

'Ow, painful! Do they really like this kind of thing?'

'They must do, we sell a lot of this stuff.'

'Well, it's expensive gear. I can't afford to buy any today, but I'll be back when I can.'

My problem was where to work from. I needed to rent a flat, but that was impossible at the moment as I was still in arrears with the mortgage and only just about making the monthly payments and paying all the other bills. I had no choice but to work from home until we sold the house, then I'd have the money to rent a separate place. It would be risky with the suspicious neighbours, though, thanks to Beulah's letter.

I had a spare room off the garage that would be ideal as it had a separate entrance, so punters wouldn't have to enter the rest of the house. It also had a toilet and shower. I was using it for storage, but all that stuff could be put in the garage. When I spoke to my partner later that evening, he was very happy with my decision to stop the sexual services. He thought my being a dominatrix an excellent idea, and with regards to the neighbours, as long as I only had two guys a day, between ten and three, we should be okay.

We set to work the next morning, when we had the house to ourselves, sorting out the spare room. Once it was empty, we positioned the dog cage, bench, school desk and easel. My partner put some hooks on the wall to hang the whips and paddles from, and some shelving to display the butt plugs. The room looked a bit spartan, but it would have to do until I earned the money to buy more equipment. My partner said he could make me a set of stocks quite quickly (he was good at making things) ready for my first customer.

I placed a new ad that read: *Mistress Truly—professional dominatrix*. Now all I could do was hope the phone would ring. I didn't know if there were enough men wanting this kind of treatment. Maybe they were few and far between. Perhaps converting the spare room had been a waste of time. I needn't have worried. When the ad came out the phone didn't stop ringing. I took two bookings for the following day at two hundred pounds each. I was so nervous I flapped about for the rest of the day, trying on various pairs of boots and shoes with the rubber dress I'd just bought.

Later, when I asked my partner how I looked, he said, 'Why are you asking me? I'm not one of your perverts.'

'I'm not accusing you of being a perv, I just want your opinion on what I look like.'

'You look fine.'

I must have looked a bit more than fine because he got the horn, bent me over the dining room table and shagged me. Then he said, 'You'd better get changed, it's nearly time to pick up the boys. You can't go dressed like that.'

As I left, he was fitting a lock on the spare room door—I didn't want the boys going in there.

After the boys went to bed, my partner suggested we watch a few mistresses in action on the computer. At least then I'd have an idea what was expected from a dominatrix. He said he'd found some sites earlier and saved them for me. Watching the various mistresses, it soon became obvious that what made a good dominatrix was her ability to act well. It wasn't enough just dressing kinky. This also applied to a certain degree to sexual services, because to entertain a complete stranger in the bedroom often deserved an Oscar, especially if the punter was utterly repugnant.

I remembered a particular client I'd visited in the Tunbridge Wells area. He was staying at his sister's house, looking after her dog while she was on holiday. He'd decided to make the most of being alone because he was still living with his parents, though he looked in his late thirties. He answered the door dressed in a bathrobe.

'Come in. It's Truly, isn't it?'

'Yes, it is. Lovely to meet you, Tony. Where would you like me to go?'

'Upstairs please, second door on the left. I'll be up in a minute. I've just got to get the dog in.'

He left me to find my own way to a typical-looking spare bedroom, with an ironing board and a pile of washing in one corner, and another piled high with unpacked cardboard boxes that had probably been there since they moved in. The bedlinen didn't match and the bedside cabinets were thick with dust, but it didn't bother me, as long as the punter was clean. Tony came up just as I was placing a couple of condoms on the bedside cabinet. He had his wallet in his hand.

Good, I thought, *I like a punter that doesn't need prompting when it comes to handing over the lolly.*

I put the one fifty he gave me in my bag, then went over to him and slipped off his bathrobe. I couldn't believe how extremely hairy he was, almost ape-like in appearance. I'd discovered a while ago that punters seemed to get far more excited if I undressed them. Maybe it was because their wives or girlfriends didn't pay them that kind of attention. Anyway, it did the trick and his cock stuck up like a tent pole. As he stood watching, I undressed in front of him, right down to my black and red basque, seamed stockings and stilettos. He couldn't take his eyes off my boobs, which were bulging out because the basque was a good ten years old and one or two sizes too small for me now.

I dropped to my knees and began to gently lick his balls with just the tip of my tongue. Then I slowly worked up to his helmet and down again. I did this several times until his balls tightened and then motioned him over to the bed. He lay on his front, which signalled he wanted a massage to make the session last longer. I started on his shoulders and neck, gently kneading his muscles, but he was so hairy my fingers kept getting tangled up. Working my way lower down his back towards his hairy buttocks, I noticed a small black lump in the crack of his bum. I suddenly realised it was a dead bluebottle fly! I wondered how long it had been trapped there, like a helpless victim in a web, and then thought I was going to have to shag this disgusting punter in a minute.

I ended the massage abruptly and asked him to roll over, slapped on a condom and jumped on. After jiggling up and down on his cock, feigning enthusiasm and faking an orgasm by shouting, 'Yes, yes!' he came, but the entire time I was thinking this was the first time I'd had a threesome in which one participant was a dead fly. That definitely deserved an acting award.

Chapter 11

It wasn't long before Mistress Truly's services were required as a dog trainer. JD (John the Dog), as he liked to be called, rang and made an appointment. He wanted to know if I was a genuine animal lover because he'd had some bad experiences. Every mistress so far had treated him cruelly: one kicked him and stubbed a cigarette out on him, another thrashed him with the lead. I told him I had two dogs and wouldn't dream of treating any animals in that way. Kind but firm, handling was the method I used to train my dogs. After a few more questions regarding feeding, toilet training and obedience, he made an appointment for the following week at twelve noon for one hour of training.

John arrived promptly, and after a lengthy chat about JD's likes and dislikes, his feeding and exercise routine, he said, 'I've brought JD's food. Would you mind giving it to him at 12.30? I'll be back in an hour to collect him, mistress. Take good care of him, won't you?'

'Yes, of course, but before you go, I'll need the training fees.'

'Oh yes, how silly of me.'

I counted out the wad of notes he'd handed me and told him, 'Yes, that's exactly right, John. Thank you, you can pick JD up in one hour.'

As soon as the transaction had been completed, John transformed into JD, complete with an over-inquisitive nose and tongue.

'Stop that, you naughty dog!' I shouted, as he tried to stick his tongue up my bottom. *Serves me right for wearing stockings, suspenders and a thong*, I thought. Dogs are dirty creatures, and always like to sniff bottoms and crutches. After sniffing around the house for a while, JD took his clothes off and left them in a pile in the bathroom. I followed him around and watched in utter amazement. This guy really thought he was a dog, or at least acted his part very convincingly.

'Come on, JD, time for your food!' I shouted, and he replied, 'Woof,' before standing up and running down the stairs towards the kitchen.

His lunch bag contained a corned beef sandwich and two dog biscuits. As I cut up the sandwich and put it in a dog's bowl, JD knelt beside me, begging with one hand and playing with his penis with the other. I was glad my partner was in the dining room and out of sight, but there in case I needed him. JD was making me feel very uneasy. His act was far too realistic, and who knew what he was capable of in doggy mode? I wondered what had happened to this man to make him want to act in this way. Maybe something awful had happened in his childhood . . . but who cared? Not me. I wasn't his analyst, and didn't want to be. After all, it was people like him that kept a roof over my head.

I placed the bowl on the floor and watched in amusement as JD ate with his arse up in the air and his head in the bowl. All he needed was a tail to complete the picture.

When he'd finished his lunch, I attached a collar and lead to his neck and said, 'Walkies, JD,' and he replied, 'Woof! Woof!'

After walking him around the house for a while, with him doing a lot of bottom sniffing, he reverted to John and asked, 'Mistress, will you relieve me?'

'Certainly not, you naughty boy. I never play with dogs' dicks. You'll have to do that yourself.'

He was obviously annoyed with my reply, because he glared and growled at me while wanking. After he came, I threw some tissues at him, calling him a dirty dog and telling him to clean his mess up. I fetched his clothes from the bathroom, and after dressing quickly he said, 'Thank you for looking after JD so well, mistress, but there's just one thing I feel I must mention.'

'What's that?'

'JD needs a lot of affection. He's a very loving dog. I'm sure you'll get it right next time he comes to see you.'

I said I would, and after saying goodbye and showing him out I found my partner giggling in the dining room.

'I'm glad you found that amusing. I didn't, he was bloody creepy.'

'You don't have to worry, I'm here.'

'Yes, I know, but I'm still not sure if I want to do that again.'

'Look, if he's willing to pay two hundred quid to act like a dog you may as well take his money, because if you don't, some other bitch will.'

Over the following weeks I saw many pathetic men that I spanked, wanked, humiliated and tortured. I'd had my shoes and boots licked clean, my body worshipped and even had a guy pay to do my housework and clean the loo with his tongue. The role of a dominatrix definitely suited me. I was being treated with respect, not having sex with any of them and getting paid well.

Chapter 12

While I was busy with punters in my new dominatrix role my partner managed to fit a new kitchen and bathroom, which nearly didn't survive. After a big argument, in which I accused him of spending too much time in chat rooms, he flew into a rage, picked up a hammer and threatened to smash up the new bathroom and kitchen unless I paid him immediately. I was so terrified in case he decided to use the hammer on me I rang my sister, told her what was going on and asked if I could borrow some money. She replied she wouldn't lend me any money for him and that she was going to call the police. I put the phone down and told him my sister was going to ask her husband for some money. Minutes later, the police knocked on the door and my partner turned into Mr Nice Guy.

He denied everything, saying, 'We were just having a little argument.'

One of the officers took me into another room and asked if I wanted him arrested.

I said, 'No, I think he understands now.' He clearly did, because he didn't mention the subject again.

I felt our luck was finally changing when, after just one week of the house being on the market, a young couple made an offer. It was only three grand less than the asking price, and as they were first-time buyers and we were moving to a rented place, I accepted. With no chain, we were able to move quickly. After paying off the mortgage and arrears totalling two hundred and fifty thousand, a couple of charging orders for ten thousand, and estate agents' and solicitors' fees, I was left with fifty-eight thousand pounds. This wasn't a fortune by today's standards and certainly not enough to buy another house. Nevertheless I was pleased, because I'd kept a roof over our heads and still had some money left.

We moved into a small two-bedroom house in another Kent town. Even though we were living in cramped conditions, I felt a huge sense of relief knowing I no longer had to entertain perverts in my own home. For a couple of months I enjoyed a normal life: neighbours talking to me instead of ignoring me and being able to walk down the road without fear of being attacked by some crazy person who'd read Beulah's letter. It was also nice to go shopping and treat myself and the boys, and not lie awake at night worrying about the bills.

But my life could never go back to being ordinary for long. I had tasted the power and excitement of working as a dominatrix and wanted more. It wasn't long before the opportunity came along for me to be able to rent a flat under a false name and without references. We were having some problems with the electrics, so the landlord arranged for an electrician to fix it. He was about sixty, with faded reddish hair, balding on top and a pasty complexion, but what he lacked in the looks department he made up for with his personality. He was so friendly and helpful, and nothing was too much trouble. He immediately set to work fitting a new socket in the kitchen, and then moved on to the bedroom. I'd been sorting out my dominatrix gear, and when he arrived it was all over the bed.

When I went upstairs to ask if he wanted a tea or coffee, he smiled and said, 'I wish I could get my wife to wear things like that.'

I laughed and said, 'I don't wear that stuff for my bloke.'

'Then who do you wear it for?'

'It's for customers.' I nearly said perverts, but then realised he could be into domination.

'Are you in photography, or modelling?'

'I wish! No, I'm a dominatrix.'

'You are joking?'

'No, I'm not.'

'What exactly do you do to these guys?' He looked at me in utter disbelief as I told him some of the things, and afterwards asked, 'Where do you work from?'

'I don't have anywhere right now because I've just moved here, but I'm planning to rent a flat locally.'

'Well, I might be able to help you there.'

'What do you mean?' I looked at him a bit warily, as I'd had guys offering their services in exchange for mine before and nothing beneficial ever came of it.

'I'm not just an electrician, I also run a letting agency in the town. What kind of property are you looking for?'

'The ideal place would have two bedrooms and its own entrance.'

'You mean something self-contained, such as a basement flat, with its own street door?'

'That would be just the ticket.'

'I have a place that would probably suit you. It belongs to a lady friend of mine who lives in Cornwall. She hardly ever visits the place, and because she's so far away she leaves me to manage everything.'

'That sounds ideal, because I can't have landlords sniffing around every five minutes.'

'You'd have to put up with me sniffing around,' he said, laughing.

'When can I have a look at the flat?'

'I have the keys at the office. When do you want to have a look?'

'Tomorrow, if possible. Say eleven?'

'Okay. I need to go back to the office and check the diary, but I think that time is fine. I'll ring you later to confirm.'

'That's great! I'd better leave you to get on with the electrics.'

After he left I thought it was all talk. It seemed too good to be true, and he was probably just horny. The moment he starts thinking with his brain rather than his cock, he'll change his mind. After all, if the owner found out that he rented me a flat, knowing what I did for a living, it wouldn't be very good for the reputation of his agency. I was taken completely by surprise when he rang back and confirmed our appointment for the next day. I jotted down the address and thanked him.

That afternoon I looked at a map and discovered the flat was right in the middle of town, in spitting distance of the shopping centre. What could be better than that? With all the hustle and bustle of people coming and going, no one would take any notice of my visitors. I was so excited at the prospect of the flat I could hardly sleep that night.

The next morning, after sorting out the family and packing them off to their various destinations, I got myself ready. I hadn't told my partner about the electrician's offer of the flat, as I wanted to keep it quiet for now. There was the possibility that if the electrician thought my partner had anything to do with my business he'd get scared and back out. After all, a guy who allowed his girlfriend to do that kind of work was usually a very unsavoury character. If I got the flat, I'd then tell my partner about it.

As I sat in my car outside the flat, waiting for the electrician to arrive, everything seemed perfect. It was situated in a busy

TALLULAH DEVERE

residential road, just off the High Street with one-hour parking, and for guys that wanted to stay longer the multi-storey car park was literally a three-minute walk away. I watched for a while and noticed how busy it was, with people constantly coming out of the properties. *No one would take any notice of my comings and goings*, I thought.

The flat itself was a basement property, with its own small flight of steps. I liked the fact that the street door was completely concealed by the steps of the flat above, so when anyone walked down and waited to be let in they couldn't be seen by neighbours or passers-by. The electrician arrived, and after greeting each other he showed me into the flat. We walked into a large hallway that was big enough to accommodate a sofa for the punters to sit on and wait. To the right-hand side of the hallway were three doors. The first led into a large bedroom with a bay window. The second was a spacious bathroom with a shower over the bath, but it didn't have a window and so smelt a bit musty. The third was a sitting room, with French doors leading to a small private garden, with a gate to the alley. At the far end of the hallway was a small kitchen. The flat was better than I'd imagined.

'How much is the rent?'

'Six fifty.'

'I'd love to take it. The only problem is references.'

'What do you mean?'

'Well, I may as well be honest, I've a terrible credit rating.'

'Can you afford to give me two months' rent in advance, plus a month's deposit?'

'Yes.'

'No problem then, that's good enough for me. When do you want to move in?'

'As soon as possible, if that's okay?'

'Okay, good. You can either pay the money direct into the agency's account or pay cash.'

'Cash is better for me.'

We shook hands and I agreed to meet him at the agency the next day to pay and collect the keys. I couldn't believe how easy it all was and felt my luck was really changing. I told my partner I'd only looked at the flat, so when I picked up the keys I asked him to come for a second look. I was pretending I valued his opinion and couldn't make an important decision like this without him. It worked a treat. After strutting around the flat he said, 'I think you should take it.'

'Do you really think so, babes?' I asked innocently.

'Yes, it's ideal.'

I'd learnt by now not to tell him more than he needed to know.

Chapter 13

I hired a transit van and we moved my things in over the weekend. The only heavy items were the bed and sofa. I didn't need a wardrobe or cabinets, as a previous tenant had left some behind. The sitting room was going to be the domination room, as I needed space to move around and it was a bit larger than the bedroom. I'd brought one of my beautiful antique iron and brass beds from home. I wanted the bedroom to look inviting and cosy, plus the bed was ideal for guys that wanted to be tied and teased.

I wasn't intending to offer sexual services myself any more, but was going to advertise for staff to handle that side of the business. It was a great pity that I'd lost contact with Gemma after the Beulah incident. I'd tried her number several times and left messages, but she never got back to me. I couldn't blame her. She probably didn't want to get involved.

While I waited for the new ad to come out offering massage and domination services, I made the finishing touches to the flat. I bought a pair of beautiful purple silk curtains and matching bedlinen plus another set of black silk bedding as a change, a black and silver bedside lamp and matching shade for the ceiling light, and some scented candles. I also bought a bundle of cream towels and a bath mat. I changed the shower curtain because the old one was smelly and mouldy.

The dom-room had all the equipment from home, plus I bought some new whips and canes, and although very expensive, I couldn't resist the Electric Stim kit. I just hoped it would be a good investment. Thanks to the generosity of a previous punter, I didn't need to buy any fetish outfits.

I'd already done a couple of cross-dressers and knew it wasn't unusual for them to bring a few pieces of lingerie, but couldn't believe it when a little man turned up with a large holdall full of brand new clothes. Not only were they still in their packaging, they were small sizes. He'd told me earlier on the phone that Cindy was happy to role-play whatever mistress chose, so instead of my favourite sissy slut training I craftily came up with the idea of Cindy as a shoplifter and myself as the female security guard. Cindy was clearly enjoying her role as a thief. Her cock was protruding out from beneath her rather short skirt as she pranced around the room in a pair of red stilettos, pretending to be shopping. It didn't take long to get a confession out of Cindy. I merely handcuffed her to the whipping bench and caned her bare arse a dozen times. After she admitted stealing the clothes, I threatened to call the police unless she handed them over to me. I then removed the handcuffs and ordered her to get dressed and leave the shop. I must admit I felt a bit guilty as I watched him walk down the street. Poor sod. The only thing I relieved him of was his heavy holdall.

By the time I'd finished the flat it looked great. All I needed now was staff, and customers of course. Back at home life wasn't going so well. I suspected my partner was up to his old tricks on the chat room sites. While celebrating my birthday over the weekend he'd received a call on his mobile. I was there at the time and he refused to answer after checking the number. This immediately roused my suspicions, especially as his phone hardly ever rang, and when it did he always answered. After a few moments he made an excuse that he needed to pop out to buy cigarettes.

I ran upstairs and watched him get in his car and make a phone call. He then drove off and returned shortly after. I decided to say nothing about the matter, as he would only deny everything and just accuse me of not allowing him to have a social life. He often said it was my fault he had no friends, when in fact even his own family had nothing to do with him. He'd apparently spent most of his childhood in a home because his father was a very violent man and took all his rage out on him. With regards to friends, my partner seemed incapable of making any, and the few times he did succeed they didn't last long.

That night, after he'd fallen asleep, I quietly got out of bed and carefully took his phone out of his trouser pocket. I crept into the bathroom so I could switch the light on. I wasn't familiar with his phone, so spent quite a while fiddling around before switching it on. He had a voicemail and a text. I was in luck—he hadn't deleted them. I checked the voicemail first: "Hi, it's Kerry here, I just have to talk to you and hear your sexy voice, and I can't wait to meet you at the end of the month. Please call me." I was so angry and shaking so much I could hardly press the buttons to read the text. How dare he think he could deceive me?

Thanks to the job I was doing I had a very low opinion of men and was now one jump ahead of a monkey when it came to their tricks. I grabbed an eyebrow pencil from my make-up bag and jotted down Kerry's number on a piece of toilet paper. After reading the text, which was similar to the voicemail, I sneaked back to bed. I lay awake for what seemed like hours, resisting the urge to smother him with a pillow, until I finally fell asleep.

The next morning I told my partner I had things to do at the flat and left him sitting at the laptop. I had the telephone number of the woman in my bag. I intended to talk to her to find out what he was up to. I politely introduced myself and said I thought my boyfriend was being unfaithful. The conversation went better than I'd expected. Kerry told me how she'd met my partner online. He apparently had a profile saying he was a single guy looking for a serious relationship. She said she was surprised by how quickly things were moving. After only a couple of weeks he began to talk more intimately. She admitted that she was flattered by the attention from such a good-looking young bloke, especially as she was an overweight middle-aged lady with four children, two of whom still lived at home.

When she told him she lived up in Warwickshire, which is a long way from Kent, he had told her: "If you love someone, distance can be overcome." He then went on to say he rented a small room in a house, and the landlady was an old woman in financial difficulties. He told her the landlady had sold the house so he had to move out anyway. He'd arranged to book into a hotel near Kerry for the weekend at the end of the month so he could spend time getting to know her more.

After hearing everything I thanked her for being so honest, and she promised me she'd have nothing more to do with my partner. In fact she'd have nothing to do with chat lines full stop; no disrespect to me, she realised she'd had a lucky escape from a creep. When I finished the call I remembered my partner once asking me how far away Warwickshire was. When I had asked why he said he'd watched something on TV and the place looked interesting. Not long after that he told me he might have some decorating work in Birmingham, and when I told him it was too far to come home each day he said he'd do it over a weekend and stop over. It all made sense now. The bastard was lining everything up so he could spend the weekend bonking her.

Whenever I spoke to him about his chat room habit and asked who he talked to for so long, he always said he was only trying to make friends, nothing else. Now I really did know different and had the evidence to face him with. I decided to wait until the evening to go back home and confront him. It would give me time to calm down a bit.

On the way home I popped into the supermarket and bought dinner and a bottle of wine. I knew I'd need a drink that night! When I got in my partner was watching TV.

'Where are the boys?' I asked with great self-control.

'They've both gone to their friends' house.'

'That's good, because I need to have a word with you.'

'Can't it wait? I'm watching TV.'

'No, it can't! I've had an interesting chat with Kerry today.'

'Who?'

'Don't give me that shit. You know I'm talking about your Internet chat room soon-to-fuck mate.'

'What did you say to her, and how did you get her number?'

'Where do you think I got the number from?'

'You fucking bitch.'

'You're so sad. Do you honestly think you're going to meet anyone worthwhile online?'

'Anyone's got to be better than being with a prostitute.'

'Do you know something? After what I've done to keep the ship afloat I deserve to be put on a pedestal and worshipped by you.'

'You're nothing but a worthless piece of shit.'

'I may be a piece of shit, but at least I'm not a parasite living off the back of someone else.'

'If I'm so bad, why are you with me?'

I'd asked myself that question a thousand times and still didn't have the answer.

I left him sitting in the lounge and went to feed myself and the dogs. I stayed in the dining room with them until the boys got home. They went straight up to their room to watch TV, and at ten I went to bed very tired and mentally drained. My partner came up to bed soon after and I pretended to be asleep. He cuddled up to me, and a few minutes later I felt his hard cock against my bottom. I lay motionless as he tried to place it between my legs. At that point I felt less for him than any punter and certainly didn't want to please his dick. I kept my legs tightly together, and after a while he gave up and fell asleep.

Chapter 14

I woke up in a positive frame of mind and told myself I couldn't afford to be upset by my partner's antics. As far as the job was concerned, I'd learnt very early on how to switch off my emotions. I now needed to do the same when it came to dealing with him.

I no longer had to do the school or college run. Henry had started work, and George was now being picked up and brought home by the school bus. This was great, as it meant more hours in the day. After they left the house I immediately switched on the work phones. I already knew the kind of response I was going to get to the massage ad, but no idea when it came to staff required. I wasn't too worried. After all, making the decision to become a dominatrix had panned out to be more profitable than selling sex, but I liked the idea of having female company in the flat. There was also the safety aspect of working alone. Up until now I hadn't run into anyone violent, but you only had to listen to the news to know this industry attracts the occasional lunatic. My partner had always been in the background; there was little choice as we lived in the same house. But it would be too risky for him to be at the flat, because if caught by the police he could be charged with living off immoral earnings (though he bloody well was). At least by having nothing to do with the flat he could deny any knowledge of it. For the time being, until I found someone, I was just going to have to take my chances.

I washed and dressed, fed the dogs and was in the middle of making a cup of tea when my partner came downstairs.

'Could I have a coffee please, love?'

I didn't reply and just looked at him.

'I wasn't really going to meet her. It was only a game.'

'Yeah, sure. And I was born yesterday.'

'Why would I want to see a fat old woman when I have you?'

'Why not? I'm old, and you once told me you prefer older women.'

'Yes I do, but they have to be sexy.'

'Look, I don't want to talk about this any more. I'm not an idiot and you can't convince me you weren't going to shag that woman if you got the opportunity. Now leave me alone, I've got things to do.'

'What things?'

'I'm going to the flat.'

'But you haven't got anyone to work with yet.'

'I don't care. I'll just do it on my own.'

'No you're not, it's too dangerous. I'll come with you, just till you find a girl.'

I didn't want another argument and so said nothing. Hopefully his services wouldn't be needed for long.

The first call of the day really got my back up, and after my partner's behaviour I was in a foul mood so I found it effortless to put the rude old sod in his place. The enquiry began with not even a good morning.

He simply said, 'What have you got?'

After replying, 'I'm sorry, what did you say?' he shouted back, 'What have you got for me?'

After calmly telling him I had a nice coconut mat with a hole in it, and because he lacked manners it was good enough for him to stick his cock in, I put the phone down. Hopefully it taught him a valuable lesson.

The rest of the day proved to be very frustrating. Guys were ringing for sex and I had to turn them down. Only one punter came along for tie and tease, at ninety pounds. My partner had become so bored by the afternoon that he went to a pub in town. He told me to ring if I got a punter and he'd be back in five minutes to look after me. A few hours later and no dom bookings, so I decided to call it a day.

While preparing dinner that night I took a call from a woman who was looking for work as a receptionist-cum-maid. I knew what the job entailed, as Gemma had spoken about the maid in Brighton where she'd worked. I took her number and promised that if I needed a receptionist in the near future I'd call her. I hadn't even considered having a receptionist until her call, but it set me thinking. It could be some time before I found someone to work with, and if I took her on my partner wouldn't have to be at the flat. After sleeping on the idea I decided to give the woman a ring and arrange an interview.

We met outside a café in East Grinstead, as it was the halfway point for both of us. Kathy was a fairly plain-looking woman, maybe a little rough around the edges but friendly enough. What did strike me as her best asset, with regards to my business, was her deep husky voice. This must have been from the vast quantity of cigarettes she smoked; she must have lit up half a dozen in the half hour I was with her. Part of her job would be to answer phones and I knew how important it was to have a good telephone voice. I'd been blessed with the ability to speak in a variety of ways, and I believe a lot of my success in this game so far was the slow sexy voice I put on for the punters. I finished the interview by saying that I'd let her know in a couple of days, although I'd already decided to give her the job.

I rang her the next morning and told her she could start anytime soon, and she said she'd be in the next day. I gave her the address and asked her to be there at eleven. When I told my partner, he said he didn't think I could afford to take on a receptionist so soon. He agreed though after I explained the danger he could be put in if the place was raided by the police.

I got to the flat the following day at half past ten so I could switch the heating on before Kathy arrived. I'd already stocked up on essentials for the fridge and cupboards, and was in the middle of a cup of tea and biscuit when the doorbell rang. I still hadn't got around to putting a curtain over the frosted glass street door, so could clearly make out the silhouette of Kathy puffing away on a cigarette.

'Come in, Kat. Oh sorry, is it okay to call you that?'

'Yeah, course.'

'I've just made tea. Would you like one?'

'I could murder one.'

We pulled up a couple of kitchen chairs and sat chatting. Kat told me all about the previous knocking-shop she'd worked in. It was in the Crawley area and run by a young woman called Emma. Before opening up the knocking-shop, Emma had been working as an independent escort. Kat lost the job because Emma wasn't making enough money. Apparently, her biggest problem was getting good reliable girls. Very often, when a girl had one or two good days earning she wouldn't show her arse for days. Flats often offered a girl just one set day a week, so there were a variety of girls to offer the punter. These kind of experienced girls were generally not prepared to give a new flat a second go if they didn't get enough punters the first day. Because of this, Emma had to go back to offering sexual services herself again in order to pay for the upkeep of the flat.

After the tea I showed Kat around the flat. She was particularly interested in the domination room.

'I think you should do really well. Not many places have this kind of equipment. We used to turn away a lot of business in Crawley because we couldn't cater for the dom punters.'

'Why didn't Emma do dom?'

'To be honest she tried, but the girls were really crap at it.'

'People don't understand the skill involved. It's not just a case of giving every punter a smack; they are all different and you have to assess each one individually.'

Just at that moment the phone rang. A customer just wanted a topless massage and hand relief, and as there was no sex involved I offered my services. While waiting for him to arrive I handed the phones (one for domination, the other for sex) over to Kat. I thought I might as well throw her in at the deep end right away. I wrote down the prices of the services and told her to burn the piece of paper when she'd memorised them. I'd remembered one of Gemma's tips: never keep a list of prices or punters' phone numbers in case the police raided.

The punter rang to say he'd arrived in town and Kat gave him the full address. I was right! Her voice and telephone manner were perfect: sexy and efficient, and not at all nervous.

She put the phone down and said, 'You'd better go and change. He'll be here in a minute.'

'Okay, take the money and count it when you let him in.'

'I shouldn't really take the money off him.'

'Why not? I'm going to have to trust you, Kat.'

'It isn't that. The law states a receptionist, or maid, whatever you want to call her, mustn't be seen to have any financial interest in the business.'

I changed and waited in the bedroom. The doorbell rang and Kat let him in. I listened at the crack of the door because I wanted to hear how she treated a punter.

'Hello, darling, do come in. Do you need to use the bathroom?'

'No thanks, love.'

'If you wait here a minute I'll just see if the lady is ready for you.'

Kathy poked her head round the door and asked, 'Ready?'

'Yes, show him in, Kat.'

While exchanging a few pleasantries I took the money off him and counted it. As I put a towel on the bed I could see this punter wasn't here for a chat, because his cock was clearly bulging in his trousers.

'Come on then, love, get your kit off and lie on the bed.'

'Can you get your tits out, darling?'

I did as he asked and let him play with them, as I knew it would make him come quicker. While he was busy playing with one of my nipples, I grabbed a tube of lubricant and squirted a drop on my hand. As soon as I started to wank him he shot his load and exclaimed, 'Sorry, love, I needed that.'

'Yes, I could tell.'

He cleaned himself with the Baby Wipes and got dressed. I needed to wash my hands, but the money was in the room so I couldn't. I wasn't going to risk him stealing it, so I'd have to wait until after he'd been shown out. Next time I'd hide the money in the kitchen before the session.

The rest of the day brought three more punters who just wanted hand relief, but I didn't complain. It was fairly easy money, apart from one guy trying to finger my fanny. I kept slapping his hand away and explaining he hadn't paid enough to do that. Eventually he gave up trying.

At the end of the day, as we were about to lock up and go home, Kat asked if we could have a TV at the flat so she could watch it when I was busy with punters. I didn't see any problem with it and promised I'd bring one the next day. I only hoped the reception would be good enough with an indoor aerial, because I hadn't noticed an outdoor one anywhere in the flat and didn't want to pay for one to be installed until I started making money. When I got home my partner wanted to know how the day had gone.

'Not too bad. We had a few customers.'

'How was what's her name?'

'She was fine. Oh, that reminds me, she's asked for a TV at the flat.'

'What does she need a television for? She's there to work.'

'You know how boring it can be just sitting around. Anyway, we can both watch it.'

'Okay, I'll sort it out for you, but in the meantime can we have dinner? I'm starving.'

I rustled up sausage, egg and chips for everyone before having a bath. I was tired and felt the need for an early night, but my partner wanted my company as he hadn't seen me all day. He insisted I sit and share a bottle of wine with him and watch a movie. After drinking one glass I was struggling to keep my eyes open, so he told me to go to bed.

Chapter 15

Over the following days very little happened, apart from a few punters wanting mild domination and one or two relief. The rest that wanted sex I turned down. It was Kat who finally took a call from a girl wanting work. She said her name was Wendy and that she was thirty-five, but she looked younger and was a size 10 with a 36D cup. When she put the phone down, Kat said she sounded a bit common (that was funny coming from her), but as we didn't have anyone to do the sex we couldn't afford to be fussy. I agreed with her, and as long as she looked okay and didn't answer the phones or talk to the punters too much she'd be fine.

Kat had told Wendy that she could do a working interview, which meant she could come for the interview and then work the rest of the day. I hadn't heard of working interviews, but Kat said that's how most flats worked. That way you were more guaranteed of the girl turning up, especially if she was skint. She also had a chance of covering her travelling costs, and maybe earning some money.

Wendy arrived at noon the next day. She had shoulder-length blonde hair and lovely big blue eyes, but unfortunately she had a very nasty scar above her lip. It looked like she'd been born with a harelip, the poor girl, but she did have a very nice figure and big boobs. I told her the prices we charged and the percentage she would receive.

'Do you think I'll get a punter today?'

'I hope so, Wendy.'

'The problem is I need to pay my sister for babysitting, and I promised the kids a takeaway tonight.'

'Don't worry, I'm sure the phones will ring soon. In the meantime, let's all have a cup of tea.'

Kat made the tea, and I opened a new tin of chocolate biscuits and put them on the kitchen table. While we sat sipping our tea, I noticed Wendy kept looking at the biscuits. I told her to help herself.

'Oh lovely, I never buy biscuits, they're too expensive.'

Kat and I watched as she ate one after another until only a few were left on the top layer. I could see by Kat's face that she wasn't impressed, especially when Wendy asked her for a cigarette.

After smoking it, she said, 'I haven't been able to afford to buy any.'

Kat replied, 'Well, when you get your first punter you can go over the road and buy some, 'cause I can't afford to keep giving them to you.' Kat then got up from the table and placed the lid on the biscuit tin. 'I'm just going to the loo. Can you answer the phones, Truly?'

'Yes, of course.' When Kat had left the room I said, 'Don't get upset by Kat, I think her bark's worse than her bite.'

'I'm sorry, Truly, but I really am skint.'

'I believe you. I've been there myself.'

'Can I ask you a favour, Truly?'

'What's that?'

'Can I borrow some condoms when I get a punter? I promise I'll replace them later.'

'Yes, of course you can.' I couldn't help feeling sorry for her. She didn't come across as the brightest spark; perhaps like many girls she didn't have much of a choice. At least this work gave them the opportunity to earn a reasonable living to support their families.

After a couple of hours of sitting around doing nothing a punter rang wanting sex, and said he was twenty minutes away. Wendy sat and applied more make-up before getting changed.

She came out of the bedroom and said, 'What do you think? I bought the bra and knickers at BHS.'

She did have a very nice figure and looked fantastic in the black lace underwear.

'You look really sexy,' I replied.

'You shouldn't have any complaints from the punter,' said Kat approvingly.

A good forty minutes passed with no news from the punter.

'Where the fuck is he?'

'I don't know, maybe he got lost.'

'He's a time-waster. You always get them, you should know that, Wendy,' said Kat.

'Yeah, I know, but I'm desperate.'

'Don't worry, it's early days, but for now you may as well get dressed or you'll get cold sitting around like that,' I said.

When she went to the bedroom to get dressed, Kat said, 'She's going to be a fucking nightmare if she doesn't get a punter.'

'I know, but what can we do?'

'There's nothing we can do. I've worked in plenty of flats and they all have days when no one walks through the door, more so when the flat has just opened up.'

'Why's that do you think?'

'It's because they've no regular punters yet. We're all just going to have to be patient, that's all there is to it.' Kat then took a book from her handbag and started reading.

I thought I'd go and check up on Wendy as she'd been in the bedroom a long time. I knocked, opened the door and found her lying on the bed.

'Are you alright, Wendy?'

'I hope you don't mind, I'm a bit tired.'

'No problem. You rest and I'll wake you up when we get a punter.' I didn't see the harm in letting her have a rest. After all, this wasn't like any other job; she was only here to please the punters, nothing else.

I was lucky, one of my old customers rang and said he'd like to see me that afternoon. When I told him where I'd moved to, he said it was even nearer for him and he'd be half an hour. David was a very wealthy old gentleman who drove a new Bentley. I remember the first time he pulled up outside my house, just after the Beulah incident. I thought then at least the neighbours could see I had high-class customers and didn't come cheap. He was a charming man who never took liberties, far from it; in fact I was the one who took liberties. He loved to be spanked and anally violated in any way I felt fit. Carrots and bananas with the skins on were favourites. David was a sucker for anything I could think of to shove up, and when it came to spanking he had no limits. I could literally spank him until he bled.

I introduced him to Kat and then took him through to the dom-room. David had bought me the usual gift of chocolates and Dom Perignon champagne. I excused myself and went to find a couple of glasses.

Kat asked, 'What are you drinking, Truly?'

'Dom Perignon, of course.'

'You're joking!'

'No, he always brings Champagne and chocolates.'

'Lucky cow. I've never tasted Dom Perignon.'

'I'll save you a drop, I promise.'

When I walked back into the room David was sitting naked at the school desk with his huge barrel-shaped belly resting on his lap.

'Stand up when your mistress enters the room!'

'Sorry, mistress. Forgive me, mistress.'

'You will open the Champagne and serve me.'

'Yes, mistress. Anything you wish, mistress.'

I waited as he carefully teased the cork from the bottle, being careful not to excite the contents. Dom Perignon was far too precious to be wasted on the carpet. As I sat sipping Champagne and eating handmade chocolates while David nibbled gently on my toes, I couldn't help thinking the life of a dominatrix was wonderful. After spanking David with a ruler and putting a toothbrush up his arse, I demanded he wank himself in my presence. As soon as he'd performed the necessary, we sat chatting as though nothing had happened. He spoke about his sons and grandchildren, and how his wife was already preparing for Christmas.

David suddenly became aware of the time, and said, 'I must go now, mistress, I don't wish to outstay my welcome.'

Just as I was showing him to the door, Wendy came out of the bedroom. I introduced them and kissed him goodbye.

'Why didn't you tell me a punter was here?'

'There was no need to. That was one of my regulars.'

'But I can do dom.'

'I'm sorry, Wendy, but your job is doing the sexual services, and you didn't mention you could do domination.'

'Anyone can do dom, it's easy money.'

Kat looked up from her book and just shook her head.

'Look, Wendy, I'll tell you what, if another guy rings for dom today you can have a go, okay?'

I thought I'd give my partner a ring to see if he was willing to bring a spare television from home and set it up so Wendy would have something to occupy her mind while she was waiting for a punter. Thankfully he agreed, although rather reluctantly. After a fair bit of swearing he retuned the TV and managed to get a reasonable picture. I was in the kitchen making coffee for everyone and heard Wendy ask him for a cigarette. I brought the coffee through to the sitting area in the hallway and found her sprawled over the sofa chatting to him.

She looked up at me and said, 'If you don't manage to nab me a punter, I'm going to have your man.'

I didn't reply as I thought she was joking, but Kat took it more seriously and said, 'You do, young lady, and you're out. Do I make myself clear?'

'I was only mucking about.'

My partner drank his coffee and left fairly swiftly. I think he was embarrassed by what had been said.

Kat came into the kitchen while I was washing up and said, 'I need to have a word, Truly.' She was talking very quietly, so I guessed it was about Wendy. 'Look, love, I know you don't have a lot of experience when it comes to running a knocking-shop, but you need to learn fast, and your first lesson is how to manage girls.'

I listened in silence as she spoke. She explained how some girls (but not all) have become desensitised when it comes to sexual boundaries and think nothing of shagging the boss's bloke. When it comes to honesty, it's a rarity. Most girls steal from the madam in one way or another. One of the easiest ways is by doing extras in the room. For instance they'll tell the madam they don't do O without, but if the punter asks in the room they tell him for extra they will. Of course the punter's not going to tell anyone about the transaction that took place in the bedroom. Another trick is asking for an advance on the next day's money. Nine times out of ten you never see the girl again.

If what Kat was saying was true of most girls, running a brothel might not be so easy. It hadn't crossed my mind that the girls might be dishonest or unreliable. Why, I don't know. After all, the job attracts desperate women. That was the reason I started.

'Kat, I have an idea. What do you think of running another ad, just for Wendy?'

'Why do that?'

'When the punters ring on the new ad we give them cheaper rates. In other words, a quickie service.'

'That's a good idea, but will she do it?'

'I don't know, but I'll go and find out.' I didn't want to exploit Wendy, so before asking her I worked out a new percentage. When I ran the idea past her she seemed very happy and promised she'd come back to work on Friday if I placed the new ad for her.

At seven-thirty that evening, having not had a single punter for Wendy, I suggested we all go home.

Wendy looked at me and said, 'But I can't get home, I've no money.'

'You're joking!' Kat asked.

'I didn't think I'd sit here all day and earn nothing.'

'If you've worked flats, you know that happens,' said Kat.

'Kat, you can help Wendy out. She lives in Crawley, you could give her a lift.'

'Yeah, I suppose so.'

'Okay, that's sorted. See you tomorrow, Kat. Wendy, don't forget Friday.'

Chapter 16

That Friday, Kat didn't share my optimism that Wendy would turn up for work as we sat sipping tea and watching the clock. The new ad was generating a lot of response. Stalling for time, Kat told punters we opened at midday and to ring back for an appointment. I thought I'd give Wendy a ring to see if she was on her way, and after several rings she answered.

'Hi, Wendy, where are you? We've got punters ringing.'

'I'm sorry, Truly, I can't come in today. I've no travel money.'

'Why didn't you ring me?'

'I haven't got any credit.'

'You could have come in with Kat.'

'I'm sorry. Maybe I can come in next week.'

'Maybe isn't good enough. I need someone I can rely on.' It seemed pointless talking to her further, so I hung up.

'I told you getting reliable girls is every knocking-shop's biggest nightmare.'

'I wouldn't mind, but I've spent money on a new ad and phone for her.'

'Don't worry, Truly, somebody else will turn up soon.'

I was in the shower when Kat took a call from a young lady named Savannah. She had Wednesday available and asked if she could do a working interview the next week. Kat took her number and told her a lady called Truly would get back to her shortly. I phoned her back as soon as I got out of the shower and wrote down her statistics and age, asking her to be here at half past ten on Wednesday.

Over the weekend I took an amusing call from a very well-spoken mature gentleman.

'Hello, am I speaking to Nurse Naughty?'

'Yes, I'm the nurse. How can I help you?'

'May I ask how old you are?'

'I'm forty-two.'

'What are your chest measurements?'

'I'm a 36D cup.'

'Do you have large nipples, nurse?'

'Yes, as a matter of fact I do.'

'Is the uniform authentic, and do you wear a nurse's belt?'

The questions were becoming tiresome and I decided to bring the conversation to an end. 'Would you like a consultation?'

'Yes please, nurse. How much is it for one hour?'

'That'll be two hundred.'

'That's fine. Can I see you on Monday, at one?'

'Yes, that's okay, but you need to ring on Monday morning to confirm you're still able to make the appointment. If I don't hear from you, I'll assume you're not coming.'

'Okay, nurse, I'll call you Monday morning. Thank you very much. Goodbye.'

Shortly after ten o'clock on Monday, the punter rang.

'Good morning, nurse, it's Donald speaking.'

'Hello, Donald. Are you ringing to confirm your appointment?'

'Yes, nurse, and I also have a request.'

'What's that?'

'Would you place two spoons in the freezer at eleven, and then at twelve-thirty transfer them to the fridge?'

'May I ask why, Donald?'

'I like to have them rubbed over my nipples, and if they're used straight from the freezer I tend to get frost burns.'

I reassured him I would follow his instructions and looked forward to the session at one. As I put the phone down I couldn't help thinking what a strange request it was, but I'd got used to punters and the weird things that turned them on.

As Kat and I sat having our first cup of tea, I told her all about Donald and his strange request. She looked at her watch.

'Have you seen the time? It's eleven thirty. You need to shove these spoons in the freezer. The problem is we don't have a freezer section in that fridge.'

'Shit! I never noticed. What shall we do?'

'Oh, just put them in the fridge. The silly old pervert's not going to know the bloody difference.'

Donald arrived at precisely one o'clock. Kat let him in and I could hear him asking if the nurse was running to time. This was a good sign, as it showed he was taking his fantasy seriously. It usually made the job easier. I shouted to Kat to show the next patient in. I was dressed in my nurse's uniform, complete with belt, black sheer stockings and high-heeled stilettos. My long, wavy golden-brown hair was tied in a bun, and I had schoolmistress-style glasses on. Donald seemed to approve of me by the way he was ogling. He was particularly drawn to my cleavage. I'd deliberately pulled the zip down before he came in, because it was obvious from the phone conversation he was a boob man.

'What's the problem, Donald?'

'I have very sensitive nipples, nurse.'

'Take your shirt off.'

He quickly removed it, and as I pulled on his nipples he let out a groan.

'Does that hurt, Donald?'

'No, nurse, it's arousing my penis.'

'I shall have to examine you.'

'Yes, nurse, I think you should, but I'd like to leave my underpants on.'

After taking off the rest of his clothes, I told him to lie down on the couch. I squeezed his balls gently through his pants and he said, 'No, nurse, please don't touch me below. It's my nipples that need treatment.'

I was beginning to wonder what I was going to do to this old man for one hour if he didn't like his cock touched, when I remembered the spoons. I called to Kat to fetch them. As she passed them through the narrowly opened door, she was trying not to laugh. I couldn't help smirking as I closed the door and went back to Donald. As I rubbed the cold spoons over his nipples, I couldn't help thinking how ridiculous it all was, but he was enjoying himself and I was being paid to humour him. The time seemed to drag by, so I decided to try and end the session a little early. I slipped my dress off in front of him and then my bra.

'Oh, nurse, your nipples are gorgeous. May I touch them?'

'Yes, Donald, if you think it will help you.'

He pulled and squeezed them quite hard. I then bent over him so my tits were in his face and suggested he suck them a little, and he replied, 'I'm sorry, nurse, but I don't like doing that.'

I thought, *what the fuck am I going to do with this man other than play with his nipples?* I then drew up a chair, sat in front of him and proceeded to play with my nipples. He watched intently and began wanking through his underpants. He then did the strangest thing: he rolled onto his side so his back was towards me and I presumed he came because his body jerked a couple of times, and then he was still. Judging by his behaviour he didn't want me to see his cock, so I passed him a box of tissues, without looking, and made myself busy tidying the room while he got dressed.

'Thank you, nurse. The treatment was successful.'

'Yes, it was, Donald. But I think you'll need more.'

'Yes, nurse, I think you're right. I'll call you when I'm in desperate need again.'

Kat showed him out, and then wanted to know all about the session.

'What the hell did you have to do with the spoons? Cos if you stuck them up his arse I'm not stirring my tea with them, that's for fucking sure.'

I laughed. 'I wish I did, the session would've been more fun. Honestly, I've never been so bored.'

'Seriously, Truly, what were the spoons for?'

'He just liked them rubbed over his nipples.'

'Is that all?'

'Yes, he was really odd. He didn't even want me to touch his dick, or see it.'

'What do you mean? He didn't show it to you?'

'No, and when he wanked he even turned his back on me.'

'What a weirdo.'

'Maybe he was shy, or had a tiny cock.'

'Who cares? He paid okay, that's the most important thing.'

Later that day we managed to grab a few more punters: one for tie and tease, one for hand relief and another for O with.

Tuesday turned out to be even more boring, with not one punter all day. By six I'd had enough and decided to close up. Kat assured me tomorrow was going to be a better day. I really hoped so. I was beginning to think running a flat wasn't worth the aggravation. After all, I made more money working from home. That evening I spoke to my partner about my concerns and he said I had to be patient. As he saw it, running a brothel was no different from any other business, and it was going to be a while before I broke even let alone made a profit.

Chapter 17

The next morning I was in the shower when Savannah rang to say she was on her way. I asked what time her train was due in and said I'd pick her up. She told me what she was wearing and I spotted her outside the station when I pulled up. I was surprised by how pretty she was, with long dark hair and a porcelain complexion, aqua-coloured eyes and a figure that looked perfect. I opened the door and waved to her. After introductions we drove to the nearby flat. I introduced her to Kat and showed her around. We had coffee, and she asked if she could change into her glamour wear.

'I like to be ready for when a punter rings. Oh, I must give you my details so you can tell them.'

While she was changing, Kat and I had a quick chat.

'She's very beautiful, Truly. Let's hope her figure is good.'

'Yes, she's quite stunning.'

'Where's she from?'

'The Czech Republic, but she's been here six years so her English is very good.'

That's when Savannah came out of the bedroom, dressed in a pink and black lacy basque, black lace-top stockings and high-heeled stilettos. Her figure was fantastic: good size boobs, a tiny waist and a pert bottom. She had everything most blokes loved.

'Do I look okay?'

'You look gorgeous. I only hope we get enough punters for you.'

'Oh don't worry, Truly. I've been doing this for six years in different flats, so I know it takes time to build up regulars. You just have to be patient, that's all.'

'I've been telling her the same thing. We've only just opened this place, so it's bound to be quiet,' Kat said.

We sat drinking tea, and Savannah told me how she came to this country six years ago to study English and worked as an au pair. But the pay was so low, so she worked one day a week at a massage parlour where her friend was also working. After a month she packed in the au pair job and worked full time offering sex. With the money she'd saved in six years she was having a house built in the Czech Republic. She then proudly showed me some photographs. I couldn't help feeling pleased for her. This young lady actually had something to show for fucking total strangers for six long years.

In the time we'd been chatting, Kat had been busy in the next room taking calls and giving Savannah's details to the punters wanting sex. She then rushed into the kitchen where we were sitting and announced excitedly, 'We have two punters! I've told one to go and have a coffee in the town for half an hour, and the other's parking up. I've given him the address.'

'What do they want?' asked Savannah.

'Both of them want a half hour, full personal.'

'Well, that's a good start to the day, Truly.'

'Yes, great. I think you've brought us luck.'

Savannah laughed and said, 'I hope so.'

The doorbell rang and Savannah ran into the bedroom. As Kat was busy on the phone, I let him in. His eyes lit up when he saw Savannah. I closed the bedroom door and listened for a few seconds. I wanted to know if she was honest. She quoted the prices I'd given her and I moved quickly away from the door as she turned the handle.

'He wants a half hour, full personal, Truly.' She handed me ninety pounds, smiled and went back into the bedroom.

After a few minutes, I could hear chatting and laughter coming from the bedroom. It was a good sign. She obviously knew how to entertain them. No sooner had he left than the next punter was at the door. I showed him in, and his response upon seeing Savannah was to ask for an hour instead. I left her to take the money and, as before, she brought out the correct amount of one hundred and fifty pounds.

At the end of the day Savannah had seen five punters and I'd had two dom guys. After giving Savannah her money, she thanked me and said, 'You're a lovely lady, Truly. Not at all like the other madams.'

'So does that mean you'll come back next week?'

'Oh, definitely. I've really enjoyed my day.'

Over the following weeks, Savannah proved herself to be a reliable and lovely girl. She managed to build up several regular punters, and had also assisted me with a couple of domination guys when they requested an assistant slave girl.

One Saturday I got to the flat early and it was a bit of a mess. I'd always considered cleaning to be a menial task, so I was delighted when a cross-dresser came along and proudly announced he enjoyed the job, and had fantasised about cleaning a mistress's domain. I put him to work dressed in a pretty black satin French maid's outfit, blonde wig, pink marigolds and a pair of size ten slingbacks I'd miraculously found on one of my shopping sprees for cross-dressers in Oxfam.

I took my hat off to him. He really did graft as I sat watching from the sofa in the hallway. The only time I lifted a finger was to smack his bottom with a large leather paddle after inspecting his work and discovering an imaginary speck of dirt. My cleaner was so conscientious in his duties that he paid for an extra half hour in order to scrub the bathroom and kitchen floor with a nailbrush. Because he'd done such a great job, I permitted him to relieve himself while still wearing the marigolds.

During the first month Savannah started working with me, a mature lady called Julie responded to the ad and asked to work as a visiting escort. After I explained to her that the job was to work in the flat, she declined to give it a try because she felt she was too old to sit in a flat all day, hoping to pick up the odd punter. I didn't want to lose the opportunity of having another lady and so I suggested she pop along for a photo shoot, and I'd then create a profile and put her on the adult work site. If any punters wanted her, they could book a time and day to meet up with her at the flat, or a place of their choice.

Julie arrived for the interview and photo shoot completely unprepared, so I lent her some lingerie and stockings. While she changed, Kat and I set to work rearranging the dom-room for the shoot. As Julie, like me, was a mature lady, I thought she would appeal to the sort of punter that likes the lady to take a dominant role. With that view in mind, I took several photos of her straddling the whipping bench holding a riding whip, taking both rear and front views. I was careful not to take any close-ups of her badly stretched thighs and bottom. Even though she was only a size eight, she told me she'd once been a size sixteen and had six children.

After looking at the photos and with Julie's approval, we chose a few to go on the website. I left Kat to create the profile and load up the pictures. When I explained the rates of pay to Julie she seemed very happy, and as she was going out the door she said, 'Promise to ring me if anyone calls. I really need the money because I haven't worked since my illness.'

'Have you been sick then?'

'Yes, I've just got over cervical cancer, but I'm all clear now.'

I didn't know what to say, so just said goodbye. After she left I thought how hard her life must be to have to resort to selling herself so soon after having cancer. If she was telling me the truth, that is. Kat said that sometimes girls give you sob stories like that, hoping you'll feel sorry for them. During the afternoon, Kat and I wrote an introduction on Julie and added it to her profile, wording it to appeal to mature men.

It wasn't until the next morning, while having our first cup of tea, that we saw the dozen or so emails Julie had received. After reading them, eight were deleted due to their requests. I'd asked Julie at the interview what she specialised in and what she didn't do. I replied to the four remaining emails and sent a phone number for them to get in contact with her. One in particular was interesting, but doubtful: a chap named Jonathan wanted two hours with her, an hour shopping for sexy lingerie and another hour having fun in the bedroom.

Two of the punters rang later in the day. Jonathan arranged to meet Julie at the flat the next day at noon. The other punter wanted an afternoon session that day. Julie was delighted when I rang and told her, but she also doubted the shopping trip. She said in all the years of working as an escort no punter had ever taken her shopping. The next day she rang at ten to twelve to say she'd arrived and was just parking up. A few minutes later, Jonathan rang for the address as he was in town.

Jonathan was the first to the flat, and as I let him in I said Julie would only be a few minutes. He asked to use the toilet, and while he was in there Julie arrived. She started taking off her coat when he came out of the toilet.

Before I could introduce them, he walked towards her and said, 'Hello there, you must be Julie. I'm Jonathan. Are you okay to go shopping, right now?'

She looked at me in disbelief for a split second, before replying, 'Yes, I'm ready, but where do you want to go?'

'Didn't Truly tell you? Lingerie shopping.'

Right after they left, Kat said, 'Lucky bitch.'

'Yes, she is, but it's good for us too. If she gets punters that pay well, she's more likely to continue working here.'

Julie and Jonathan got back at one, carrying a couple of La Senza shopping bags. Julie showed him into the bedroom before emptying the bags in front of us. Her punter had certainly been generous. She'd been allowed to choose several different outfits, from basques to matching bras and knickers and suspenders. The receipt was for three hundred and twenty pounds.

I told her to change into one of the outfits as quickly as she could so as not to keep him waiting too long. She changed into a black and pink polka-dot basque and matching knickers and then went into the bedroom. A few moments later she came back into the kitchen and handed me three hundred pounds.

'Make sure you treat him well. Punters like that are hard to find.'

'Don't worry, Truly, I know how to look after him.'

While Julie was busy with Jonathan, her other punter rang to say he was on his way. Kat told him not to arrive before two thirty, as we didn't want the punters running into each other. We tried to respect the fact that even punters liked to think the girl belonged to them, if only for an hour or so. At ten past two the bedroom door opened and Jonathan came out, followed by Julie. He kissed her goodbye and left.

'Thank God that's over. I'm dying for a cup of tea and a fag.'

'Sorry, Julie, you haven't got time. Your other punter will be here soon.'

'You're joking?'

'No, I'm not, so go tidy up in the bedroom and don't forget to spray some air freshener around. There's nothing worse than a punter being able to smell the previous one.'

Her next punter was much younger than her. He probably fancied older women. Kat showed him into the bedroom while Julie freshened up in the bathroom before going in to him. She then poked her head out the door, waving the money. Kat took it off her and brought it to me in the kitchen.

'She's doing okay for someone that's a bit past her sell-by date.'

'Now, now, Kat. We're not exactly spring chickens.'

'Yes, but that one rates herself.'

I'd no intention of getting drawn into Kat's little game of bitching about the girls. It was hard enough to find staff without making them feel uncomfortable while working here. I knew if Kat continued to do this I'd have to have words with her.

'Kat, can you please check the emails while I make us something to eat?'

'Some guy wants an outcall tonight at nine, and another wants a couple of hours tomorrow afternoon. He's left his mobile number for her to call.'

'Give me the number, Kat, and I'll call him. I'll just pretend I'm her.' I rang and spoke to a very nice-sounding man, who wanted a two-hour session at the flat tomorrow at one. I then sent an email to the guy who wanted the outcall, asking him to call me a.s.a.p.

Julie was happy to do the outcall, as long as she could go home for a while to make sure everything was okay and that her partner had fed the kids. When I asked how old they were, she said four were grown up and the other two were teenagers still living at home.

When Julie was ready to leave, I handed over her money. She checked the amount and said, 'Not bad for a few hours work.'

'Yes, it's good, especially if you count the bag of goodies.'

That evening, the punter wanting the outcall rang to confirm and gave his address. I texted Julie the details and told her to bring my cut of the money the next day.

Chapter 18

The next day, Julie was fifteen minutes late for her one o'clock appointment and I had a difficult job convincing him to wait.

'Are you sure she's on her way?'

'Yes, I'm sure. She rang just before you got here to say she was coming.'

'Well, if she's not here in ten minutes I'll have to go.'

I'd learnt early on that if you kept a punter waiting you risked losing him. Maybe it gave them time to develop last-minute nerves, or guilt. After what seemed like an eternity, Julie arrived and took him straight into the bedroom. An hour and a half later she came out in her knickers and bra and I asked, 'Is everything okay?'

'Yes, Truly, the gentleman is just leaving.'

She left Kat to show him out and disappeared back into the bedroom. A few minutes later she came into the kitchen, where Kat and I were making tea.

I sensed a problem and asked, 'Was he difficult?'

'No, not at all. He didn't even want sex.'

'Why didn't you bring the money out?'

'I just wanted to get him over and done with, and I need to talk to you about the money.'

'What's the problem?'

'Well, I'm not happy about the sixty per cent forty per cent arrangement; I think you take too much.'

'You were happy about it yesterday,' said Kat.

'Look, Julie, when you started yesterday I told you I take sixty per cent.'

'But I'm doing all the work.'

At that point I began to lose my patience. 'I think you're the greedy one, Julie, not me. After all, I get you the work and you've used my premises. If you're not happy I suggest you leave, but before you do, don't forget you need to give me last night's money as well as today's.'

She reluctantly handed it over and Kat counted it as I showed her out.

'I'm really sorry you feel like this, Julie. Good luck.'

As soon as I closed the door, Kat started. 'What a fucking ungrateful old cow! She's lucky you even employed her at her age.'

'What I can't understand is why she was over the moon yesterday and not today.'

'I'm afraid to say it, Truly, but you're going to meet a lot more like that. And even worse.'

For the next couple of weeks, apart from having the Wednesday covered by Savannah, I couldn't find another girl to handle the sexual services. I was getting the occasional dom guy, but that wasn't enough; I had the overheads on the flat to pay as well as Kat's wages. I decided I'd have to do sex again, hopefully for a brief period, until we managed to find a reliable girl.

When I told Kat, she said, 'Well, you've done it before, so it's not going to hurt to open your legs again for a while, is it?'

'No, I suppose not.'

'Look at it this way, Truly, you give it to your boyfriend for free, better to get paid. I only wish I could charge for my body.'

Then laughing, she said, 'Cheer up, Truly, what's another cock or two at your age?'

I started laughing as well. She was right, even if she had put it crudely.

So for a couple of weeks I shagged every punter that came through the door with enough cash. I told Kat not to sell me for any less than eighty pounds over the phone, and to lie a bit about my age. The experience wasn't altogether unpleasant, because one of my favourite punters from the days when I was offering sex came to see me. He was a lovely guy and a great fuck. He really was in the minority of punters that I actually enjoyed. I think it was because he was good fun, and I felt totally at ease in his company.

I also had a really good domination session with a bloke called Keith. He first rang and spoke to me one afternoon while Kat had popped out to get lunch. He said he was an experienced slave and had visited mistresses, on and off, for twenty-five years. He then ran through a list of things he'd done over the years and was willing to try anything new I wanted to inflict on him. He asked for an appointment for the following day at noon.

As I tidied the dom-room prior to his appointment, I tried to think of something new to perform on slave Keith. It would be okay to repeat some things, but for the finale it must be a first, especially if I wanted him to come back again. After tidying up, I got ready for him, squeezing into a black rubber minidress and putting on a pair of black high-heeled stiletto boots. Kat returned just as I was applying make-up.

'You look great, Truly, but I think you need more eyeliner, and change the pink lipstick to red.'

I was just finishing this when the doorbell rang.

'I'll get it, Kat.' I grabbed a riding whip and opened the door. 'Come in, slave Keith.'

He dropped to his knees, exclaiming, 'Oh, Goddess.' He then proceeded to kiss my boots.

'Get up off your knees, slave. The session doesn't begin till I receive my tribute.'

'I'm sorry, mistress, I couldn't help myself. You're so beautiful.'

I grinned and wondered how many times he had said those same lines. I counted his money and then led him into the dom-room by his ear.

'Wait there till I return, slave.'

'Yes, mistress.'

I had a pee and hid the money in the bathroom before returning.

'Take your clothes off in my presence, you unworthy creature. I want to look at your pathetic body.'

'As you wish, mistress, I am at your mercy.'

'You have the body of a slug: white and untoned.'

'I'm sorry, mistress, if I disgust you. I deserve to be punished.'

I began the punishment with a good hard flogging to his backside with my riding crop, while riding him around the room on his hands and knees with a leather bridle complete with a rubber bit. I then removed the bridle and allowed him to lick my boots, before placing him in the stocks.

He watched as I buckled up a strap-on and applied a squirt of lubricant, and said, 'Mistress, please be gentle with me.'

'Who gave you permission to speak, slug?'

'I'm sorry, mistress.'

I went behind him and grabbed his hips. After a couple of failed attempts, the rubber cock disappeared up his arse, he let out a groan and I knew I was in. I then grabbed the back of his hair with one hand and kept the other on his hip. I fucked him hard and deep for several minutes until he muttered the safe word that I'd given him at the beginning of the session. A safe word is used to say 'stop' in an unmistakable way during the session.

'You're a wimp.'

'Sorry, mistress.'

'Now lie on the floor with your hands behind your head, and spread your legs.'

As he did as he was told, I handcuffed him and stood over him with a lit candle.

'Oh no, mistress, not hot wax.'

I took my knickers off and shoved them in his mouth. 'This is so I don't have to hear your pathetic whining.'

He squirmed and flinched as I poured hot wax over his cock and balls. I then released the cuffs and made him lean over the whipping bench.

'What are you going to do to me now, mistress?'

'Shut up, slug. You'll find out soon enough.' The truth was I still didn't know what to do to him. 'I'm going to restrain you in case you have any ideas about escaping.' Once I'd restrained him to the bench, I left the room for a five-minute tea break. Kat looked at me and said, 'Have you finished with him yet?'

'No, he's tied to the bench.'

As I watched Kat puffing away on a cigarette, I thought of an idea to finish the session. 'Kat, can I have one of your cigarettes please?'

'Yes, help yourself.'

I walked back into the room and lit the cigarette in front of him with the candle. I took a drag and blew the smoke in his face. 'You are now going to smoke it, slug.'

'As you wish, mistress.' He pouted his lips in anticipation.

'Oh no, silly, you're not going to smoke it with that hole.'

I then parted his cheeks and placed the cigarette in his bottom. 'Now, pull in your bottom muscles like you're holding in a poo.' After he had done that a few times I removed the cigarette and commanded, 'Now push like you're having a poo.'

I couldn't believe it, but little puffs of smoke came out of his bottom. He also saw it, as he was facing a full-length mirror. I then popped the cigarette in his mouth, quickly released him from the bench and ordered him to wank. As he was coming, he spat out the cigarette and shouted, 'Oh, Goddess!' When he'd recovered and regained his composure, he looked at me and said, 'You are a true goddess. In all the years I've been visiting mistresses I've never been ordered to smoke a fag with my arse.' He then fell to his knees again and kissed my hand.

'I'm glad you enjoyed the session, Keith, and hope to see you again.'

'Oh, mistress, I will definitely be back again.'

I left him to get dressed and told Kat to show him out when he was ready. When he'd gone we fell about laughing as I described, in great detail, what I'd subjected him to.

'Oh, Truly, I wish I could have seen that.'

'I couldn't believe it myself. Who'd have thought the smoke could have been exhaled, let alone inhaled?'

'I've got to say, Truly, you're a fucking good dominatrix.'

'Yes, I'm not bad, am I? Mummy always said I was a born actress and should have been on the stage.'

'Your mum was right. You'd have made a bloody fortune.'

The rest of the day passed very slowly with only two punters. One wanted half an hour personal service and the other a topless massage with hand relief. Just as we were about to go home, the phone rang.

'If it's a punter wanting sex, tell him we're busy.'

'I don't mind stopping, Truly.'

I laughed and said, 'That's up to you if you want to shag him. I'm going home.'

She was still laughing as she answered the phone, and after a few seconds I realised it wasn't a punter but a girl looking for work.

'Pass the phone over, Kat.'

I liked the sound of the young lady. She was well spoken and confident, and if her description of herself was true, very attractive. I arranged to meet her in a pub in town for an interview the next day at eleven thirty.

Chapter 19

Brooke hadn't lied about her looks. She was really lovely. The first thing I noticed when she walked into the pub was her beautiful long, dark corkscrew hair. That wasn't her only asset: her face was very pretty with velvet-brown eyes, and judging by the skin-tight jeans and jumper she wore, her body was great.

I ordered a couple of coffees and she told me that her experience ranged from strip clubs to massage parlours.

'Have you ever done any domination?'

'No, but I'd love to try it.'

I told her that if she came to work for me I'd teach her. Because of her confident manner she'd make a convincing mistress, even though she was only twenty-five years old. I invited her to visit the flat before making any decisions about taking the job. After having a look around the flat and a chat about the rate of pay, she asked if she could work every day.

'I was hoping you'd ask that, because apart from Savannah on Wednesdays I don't have anyone else.'

'I can start tomorrow, if you like.'

'That's great. I'll see you at eleven.'

Not only was Brooke a confident and highly capable young lady, she was also good fun. She was able to entertain the punters in the bedroom, as well as being a very formidable mistress. Over the following weeks leading up to Christmas we all worked hard and the flat was making a small profit. But no matter how many new ads and numbers I placed, Kat and I noticed that apart from one or two new voices, the same punters rang using the same old banter. I came to the conclusion that because we were working in a relatively small town, there just weren't enough punters per population.

Savannah suggested having a couple of new girls instead of Brooke every day, because punters liked variety. I didn't want to upset Brooke and risk losing her. Apart from her bad habit of sometimes turning up late, she'd never let me down. So I decided I'd advertise for another girl to work in the flat on the same days as Brooke and Savannah. That would give the punters a choice, and hopefully the girls would still earn okay.

Brooke didn't have a problem about the possibility of having to work with another girl. As she saw it, punters were more likely to come along if told they had a choice of girls, so it was possible she could earn even more. Savannah, on the other hand, wasn't happy. She pointed out that she'd built up several regular punters who liked to catch up with her on Wednesdays, so asked if I could let her have the day to herself. I agreed, as she'd proved to be a good earner on her own up until then.

I saw only one problem with having two young girls working in the flat on the same day: the neighbours might become suspicious, and if the police did pay us a visit it would be hard to deny I was running a brothel.

Over the weekend I made another difficult decision. If I were to survive I needed to make cutbacks, and the only way I could do that was to lay Kat off. Deep down I knew I should have done it a long time ago, because she had started to take too many liberties with me. Ever since starting the job Kat's family were constantly ringing her mobile from morning until evening, sometimes spending up to half an hour chatting about unimportant things.

When I had words with her about it and suggested she switch it off and just use it in her break-time, she said, 'My Vince will worry if my phone's turned off.'

There was also the bingo online. I made a big mistake letting her use the laptop at lunchtime for her little flutter. Had I known earlier that she was addicted to it I'd never have allowed it.

The opportunity to dismiss Kat arose that Monday morning. After arriving half an hour late, she didn't ask but announced that she would have to go home after lunch to take her husband to get his car taxed.

'Why can't he do it himself?'

'Oh, he can't read or write.'

'What do you mean?'

'He's dyslexic, and he needs my help.'

'If that's the case, why didn't you do it before you came to work?'

'He was still in bed.'

'Look, I'll tell you what, why don't you go now?'

'Oh, are you sure you don't mind, Truly?'

'I'm sure, as long as you don't come back.'

'Are you giving me the sack?'

'Yes, here's your money, now go.'

Brooke turned up a few minutes after Kat had gone. When I told her what had happened, she said, 'Serves her right for taking the piss.'

She then asked to have the week off leading up to Christmas, but as it was only two weeks away it didn't leave me much time to find a girl to cover for her. Fortunately, Savannah came to the rescue by contacting a friend of hers who worked in Brighton. Jasmine jumped at the chance to work over the festive season; the madam she worked for always closed for a two-week holiday and Jasmine couldn't afford to go without money for that long. I knew nothing about Jasmine, but Savannah assured me she was a twenty-four-year-old Russian, very sweet natured and reliable.

Jasmine arrived at the flat somewhat bedraggled, as she'd got caught in a downpour walking from the station.

'Come in, Jasmine, and warm yourself in front of the fire while I make you a warm drink. You look freezing.'

'Thanks, Truly.'

I wondered why she didn't have a warm coat on in December when she had to use public transport. As I walked through from the kitchen, she was standing by the radiator on which she'd placed her boots and socks to dry.

'Have they got very wet?'

'They have a hole in the sole, so my socks are wet.'

'I think you need a new pair of boots.'

'Yes, certainly in this weather.'

'Well, maybe later I can take you to the shopping centre and you can buy a new pair to go home in.'

She didn't comment but just smiled at me. I didn't want to embarrass her so I changed the subject.

'Did it take long for you to get here?'

'No, a little more than an hour.'

'So it's not a problem getting here and working over the Christmas period?'

'No problem.'

Towards the end of the day I asked Jasmine what time she wanted to go home. Her reply surprised me, as she asked if she could sleep at the flat.

'Why do you want to sleep here?'

'My boyfriend won't pick me up.'

'But you've earned okay, so you can make your own way home.'

'Yes I know, but please let me stay here.'

'Okay, as long as you promise not to open the door to anyone but me.'

After insisting she phone me if there were any problems, I wished her goodnight. As I drove home I felt a terrible sadness for her. Something wasn't right, but it wasn't my business to pry. After all, she was a grown woman and I wasn't forcing her to do anything against her will.

The next morning I arrived at the flat a bit earlier than usual and found Jasmine fast asleep. As the phones hadn't started ringing yet, I let her sleep for another hour and a half. I was in the kitchen making toast when she woke up.

'Truly, I didn't hear you come in. Why didn't you wake me up?'

'It's no problem. The phones haven't rung yet.'

'Yes, but I need to get ready.'

'Did you sleep well?'

'Yes, very well thanks, it's a nice warm flat.'

'Do you want some toast?'

'Yes, please.'

After having breakfast, Jasmine got herself ready. While she was in the shower, the phone rang. It was a regular punter enquiring if I had a new girl.

'Yes, as a matter of fact I do.'

'Oh lovely, can I make my way over?'

'Yes, of course. You know where we are.'

'I can't wait. See you soon.'

I had a strong dislike for this kind of punter, because they nearly always had a little moan about the girl after they'd had her. Not usually on the first visit, but the second. The girl was merely regarded as a piece of flesh that he'd paid to please him.

When I first started offering sex I took it personally if a punter complained, or worse still came to the door, looked at you and then made a rude comment like, 'You're too old,' or

'You're too fat', or 'No, sorry, you're not what I'm looking for.' Even though I'd become immune to such comments, I tried to protect the girls from that kind of abuse. I knew how much it could hurt, especially if the girl was feeling low or insecure.

We had a busy few hours, and late in the afternoon I suggested to Jasmine that we take a break from the flat.

'I've some Christmas shopping to do. Why don't you come with me and get yourself a pair of boots?'

'No, I can't do that, Truly.'

'Why not? You've worked hard, treat yourself.'

'I'd love to, but my boyfriend won't like it.'

'What's it got to do with him?'

'He's meeting me tonight to pick up some money.'

'Is your boyfriend a pimp?'

She didn't answer my question so I dropped the conversation. Instead, I told her to have a little rest while I popped into town.

Armed with a shopping list I'd made earlier, I made a beeline to the appropriate shops. I didn't have time to wander around aimlessly as time was money for myself and even more so for poor Jasmine. I was certain she was being pimped. As I let myself into the flat I could hear Jasmine arguing with someone on her mobile. I went to the kitchen to make a cup of tea, and after a few minutes she walked in.

'Is everything okay, Jasmine?'

She hesitated before saying, 'Can I talk to you?'

'Yes, of course.'

She told me how she'd come to this country to find work, and after being here a few weeks she'd met an Albanian man. He introduced her to a friend of his who worked in a massage parlour in Brighton. The Albanian began a relationship with Jasmine and soon found her a bedsit to rent so she could move out of the hostel she was staying in. When she told him she couldn't pay the rent and didn't want to take the bedsit, he told her he loved her and that he'd pay the rent. A week after moving in he asked her for money and suggested she work in the massage parlour. Reluctantly, she agreed.

'What happens if you don't give him money?'

'He hits me, and threatens to phone my parents and tell them what I do.'

'You have to get away from this man. He's dangerous.'

'I'm trying to. That's one of the reasons I came to work here over Christmas.'

'But you said he was meeting you tonight.'

'He doesn't know the address. I'm just going to meet him in town and give him a hundred pounds. That way he'll leave me alone for another day so I've got time to plan where I'm going to go.'

'Do you want me to go with you?'

'No, Truly, I'll be okay, but thanks for offering.'

I waited for her to come back from her meeting with the Albanian before going home.

Jasmine was having breakfast when I arrived the next morning.

'Good morning, Truly, I hope you don't mind me eating some cornflakes and toast?'

'Don't be silly, it's there for everyone. Anyway, how are you?'

'I'm okay. I've managed to sort things out.'

'What do you mean? How have you sorted things?'

'A friend is going to pick me up here tomorrow as it's my last day, and then take me back to my flat so I can pick up my stuff.'

'And then what?'

'We're going to Birmingham.'

'Who's this friend?'

'He was a friend of my boyfriend, but they fell out.'

'Does this guy know what you do?'

'Yes, but he's promised to help me find work in Birmingham.'

'Doing what?'

'The same thing.'

'You silly girl, Jasmine. He'll do the same thing as your boyfriend.'

'Oh no, Truly, he's a nice man.'

'Look, Jasmine, take it from me, any man who encourages or allows his partner to do this, or worse lives off her, is not a nice man. Trust me! I know what I'm talking about.'

'Don't worry, Truly, I'll be okay.'

'Can I give you a few words of advice, for what they're worth? If you have to do this job do it for yourself and not for any other bastard.'

I had to admit, after talking to Jasmine I felt like a complete hypocrite. I too had a relationship with a bastard, so perhaps I should practise what I preached.

Chapter 20

Christmas was a welcome break from the flat and the atmosphere at home was lovely for a change. My partner acted more excited than the boys. He decorated the tree, and when he discovered I hadn't managed to buy any chocolates to hang on it he immediately went on a quest to find some. He eventually returned, two hours later, with several packets, and after hanging them on the tree he insisted we wrap the presents and put them underneath.

The boys couldn't believe how many presents there were, and I also hadn't quite realised until I saw them all under the tree, but I was happy to be able to spoil the boys that Christmas. After eating and drinking too much, and seeing in the New Year, I was ready for work.

I sent Brooke a text and the reply came back, *I'm skint, so when shall we start? x.* I replied, *tom.* Considering it was the second of January we did manage to pick up a couple of punters. Brooke and I laughed; they were probably fed up with spending so much time with the wife and relatives over the holidays, and were dying for a bit of entertainment. Or maybe they hadn't had much luck scoring at the office party, so they decided to pay for a shag instead.

The rest of the day dragged and we sat chatting about our previous experiences in other areas. I admitted that mine were very limited, as the only other place I'd worked from was my last home and so far it had been more profitable than this place. Brooke, on the other hand, had worked in many parts of the country, and the one place that interested me the most was London, W1. I had been thinking about London for several weeks and the possibility of moving the business there. Brooke certainly made it sound attractive: no shortage of punters or girls, and even the police were more tolerant, as long as you didn't cause any disruption to the neighbours. One day, when she was working at a flat in London, she told me the police paid a visit. They were very polite, and after a chat with the girls and receptionist they left them in peace. It all sounded too good to be true, but maybe the streets of London were paved with gold as far as the sex industry was concerned. I was yet to find out, but for the time being I had to put my efforts into making this flat a success.

So I placed a new, larger ad in the paper for staff, and shortly after it came out a young lady called Judy phoned. Her voice sounded tired and dull like an old person's, not at all what you'd expect from a twenty-four year old. But after describing herself I decided to at least meet her.

The following day I left Brooke at the flat for an hour, as I'd arranged to meet Judy at a pub. I was just finishing a coffee when I spotted her walking in. Her figure was tiny, no more than a size six, almost childlike in stature, and she had blonde shoulder-length hair. I attracted her attention with a small wave and she smiled as she walked towards me. As she came closer, I became aware of her beauty: she had huge come-to-bed eyes, a cupid-shaped mouth, pale complexion and not a hint of make-up. She reminded me of a young Kylie Minogue.

'Would you like a drink, Judy?'

'Could I have a rum and coke, please?'

I gave her the money to get her own drink, and after settling herself down we began the interview.

Judy told me all about her previous place of employment, and how the girls and madam were very unkind and bitchy towards her. I assured her that none of that went on in my flat and every girl was treated equally. She seemed keen to see the flat, so after she'd necked another rum and coke I asked her to come and have a look. As we walked to the flat I told her about Brooke, who was holding the fort.

Brooke was her usual bubbly, friendly self and made Judy feel very welcome. After being shown around the flat and discussing the rates, Judy asked, 'Who does the domination?'

'I do, and sometimes Brooke assists me.'

'Can I have a go?'

'Yes, I don't see why not, if a guy wants you.'

'Oh great, I've always wanted to be a dominatrix.'

I didn't reply, but thought Judy didn't really have what it took to be a mistress. Not only was her frame too frail but her voice was monotonous, and as domination required a high level of acting I felt she wouldn't be any good. Nevertheless, I didn't want to upset her at this stage.

Judy promised to send a text later to let me know what day she could start. She said she had to make up a suitable lie to her boyfriend because he didn't know what kind of work she really did. I told her I had no problem with that, as long as she didn't expect me to lie to him on her behalf if he ever questioned me.

Brooke's husband was also unaware of what she did, but so far she had successfully kept it from him. The last thing I wanted was some irate partner banging on the door and accusing me of leading his woman astray.

On Judy's first day I asked her if she was okay about doing a photo shoot and she replied, 'As long as you don't show my face I don't mind.'

'Before I put them on the website, I promise I'll blank out your face.'

'I hope so, cos I don't want my family to find out again.'

'Again?'

'Oh don't worry about it, Truly, it was a long time ago.'

'What happened?'

It was hardly surprising that Judy looked and sounded tired of life after she told me her life story. She'd been sexually abused by her stepfather at the age of ten and kept it a secret for six years. When she told her mother, instead of believing her daughter she accused her of being a liar and threw her out of the house. Judy slept rough for a few days before an older man called Frank befriended her and took her in. He fed her and in return she repaid him with sexual favours. At first he just wanted her to wank him, but one time he forced her to suck his smelly penis. When she heaved and retched, he just grabbed the back of her neck, forcing himself further down her throat until he came in her mouth.

The abuse took a turn for the worse one evening. Judy was in her attic room when she heard a knock at the door. She thought it was a bit strange, as the old man rarely had visitors and never at night. For the next hour or so she could hear talking and laughing coming from downstairs. Then heavy footsteps sounded on the stairs and her door was flung open. Frank stood swaying slightly and held onto the doorframe for support, the stench of stale body odour and whisky even more overpowering than usual.

'Come downstairs, Judy, there's someone who'd like to meet you.'

'I'm not feeling very well, Frank, can I meet him some other night?'

'If you want to curl up in that warm bed tonight instead of spending it on the street, you'd better come downstairs and meet my friend.'

Tears filled her eyes as she told me how they subjected her to sexual abuse. They took it in turns to hold her down and fuck and bugger her. At the end of the ordeal she was told to go and clean herself up. As she left the room, the other man shoved a twenty-pound note in her hand.

What happened that night wasn't a one off, but became a regular Friday night occurrence. But instead of dreading it Judy came to look forward to it; not for the sex act, but for the payment. Money meant options, and options meant a way out. After managing to save three hundred pounds that she'd hidden in a sock behind the radiator, she waited for Frank to have his afternoon nap and left.

After sleeping rough for a couple of nights and spending the days hanging around an indoor shopping arcade, a young woman approached her and asked for a light. They chatted for a while and the woman invited her to join her for a coffee. It wasn't long before Judy poured out her story, and after hearing it the young woman confessed she worked part-time in a flat. If Judy wanted she could ring the madam and ask if she needed staff. That day Judy started working at the flat.

Things went well for a while. Judy worked most days and had managed to find a room to rent through a friend of the madam, but it all ended when the police raided the flat. Judy had lied about her age to the madam, but the police weren't so easily fooled. After getting her full name out of her they ran a check and discovered she'd been reported missing. Because she was under eighteen, her parents and Social Services were told what she'd been doing.

After listening to her story I realised I had to take every care that whoever I employed was old enough, and the only way of being sure was to insist on seeing some form of photographic ID. As if Judy had read my mind, she pulled a passport out of her bag and placed it on the table.

'That all happened a long time ago, Truly.'

I looked at the passport and handed it back.

'The only thing I worry about now is my boyfriend finding out, cos he'd kill me.'

We'd just about finished the photo shoot when the phone rang. Brooke answered and described both herself and Judy. As soon as she put the phone down it rang again and this time I answered, giving the girls' details. The punter was particularly interested in Judy. When I asked if he'd visited us before he said no, but he'd rung several times. He was interested in a particular type of girl and what I'd described before certainly wasn't what he wanted.

The first punter that phoned turned up half an hour later and chose Brooke, much to Judy's disappointment. I told her not to worry, as the day had only just begun. Her face was sullen the whole time Brooke was busy and I started thinking she was going to be like Wendy, but as I couldn't force a punter to choose her, she'd just have to lump it.

Shortly after I let Brooke's punter out the next one arrived. I showed him into the bedroom and told him the girls would be in to meet him very soon. Judy was taking ages in the bathroom, so I let Brooke meet him first. She was in the bedroom for no more than ten seconds before the door opened.

'He wants to see Judy. He says I'm not his type.'

A few seconds later Judy finally emerged from the bathroom and I told her, 'Hurry up, the man's waiting.'

She was in the bedroom for a good few minutes before coming back out. Judging by her big smile he'd chosen her.

'What does he want, Judy?'

'He wants an hour.' She handed me the money and trotted back to the bedroom. After a few minutes, she came back out again.

'What's the problem?'

'He wants me to dress younger.'

'What?'

'He wants me to look like a little girl.'

'I knew he was a pervert. I'm fucking glad you got him,' said Brooke.

'What shall I wear, Truly?'

'The only thing I have is a school uniform, but it'll be way too big for you.'

She put the shirt on and rolled up the sleeves while I pleated the skirt at the waist and pinned it with a couple of safety pins I had in my handbag.

'Button the shirt right up and put a tie on. It's obvious he doesn't want to see your tits. He wants you to look prepubescent,' Brooke said.

'Fuck off, Brooke,' said Judy.

'Just hurry up and get your arse back in there, before he decides to walk.'

'Okay, Truly.'

While Judy was busy, I expressed my concerns to Brooke about the punter. It was the first time I'd come across his sort, and I admitted I wasn't comfortable about it. Brooke tried to reassure me that he probably just fantasised about little girls, and as long as that's all he did it wasn't a problem. But I was worried and couldn't help thinking what if, in some way, we were encouraging him?

Judy was still in the bedroom with the punter when I noticed his time was up. I was eager to get rid of him, so I banged on the door.

'I'm sorry, Judy, but his time's up.'

'It's okay, Truly, the gentleman is about to leave.'

As I showed him out, I refrained from telling him to stay away and said instead, 'Thank you, and I hope you enjoyed yourself.'

He grinned and replied, 'I did, thank you; she's a lovely little girl.'

'What did the creep want to do?' asked Brooke.

'He wanted me to pretend he was the headmaster and it was my first day at school.'

'What else?'

'That's it really.'

It was apparent Judy didn't want to talk about what had gone on, so the subject was dropped.

The rest of the day went well; both girls had a few more punters and I received a dom booking for the next day from a bloke called Phil. He said he was a novice and would like to try mild domination. His voice sounded familiar and I was sure he was an old customer from my previous house. I didn't describe myself in case he didn't want to see me again. I thought it best to wait for his reaction, and if he didn't want me he had a choice of two other girls.

Chapter 21

Phil arrived bearing Champagne and chocolates (another one!). My memory hadn't let me down. He was one of my old punters, and judging by the way his eyes lit up he was pleased to see me. In fact, he was one of my earliest punters, and I remembered he was full of excitement throughout the session.

'Hello, Phil, how lovely to see you.'

'Oh, Mistress Truly, I was hoping it was you, that's why I've brought these gifts.'

'Thank you, Phil. That's very kind.'

Phil was a very well endowed guy, and it looked as though it was about to burst through his zip at any moment. I grabbed his bulge and led him through to the dom-room.

'Now what would you like, Phil?'

'Whatever you like, Mistress Truly.'

'Well, I have a little surprise for you. Now wait here while I fetch it.' I left the room and placed the Champagne and chocolates in the kitchen, where Brooke was sitting munching on a bag of crisps.

'Oh lovely, Truly, Champagne and chocs.'

'We'll drink that later, but first I want you to meet Phil. I'm sure we can fleece him if we offer a double act.'

'I need to change first.'

'Don't worry about it, Brooke, just go in with your knickers on.'

Phil was standing in his underpants when we walked into the room.

'Look at the naughty boy, Brooke, his cock is already stiff.'

Brooke performed right on cue. She walked over to him, pulled his pants down, dropped to her knees and gave his penis a quick suck. She then got up and calmly walked out of the room. That brief performance was enough to make Phil easy pickings.

He handed over three hundred pounds for the session without hesitation, and for the next hour we tortured and teased him until he begged for relief. It was at that point I fitted him with a collar and lead, and Brooke walked him into the bedroom. She then commanded him to lie on the bed, face up, and we blindfolded him and tied his hands and feet to the bedposts. I sat on his face while Brooke rolled a condom onto his rock-hard cock. She then gave him a blow job and it was over in a few seconds.

'Wow, ladies, that was amazing!'

I went to fetch his clothes while Brooke released him from the bed before leaving the room. She came to the door as I was showing Phil out and he kissed us both on the hand, and said, 'Thank you, ladies, for giving me such a great time.'

'It's a pleasure, Phil. We hope to see you again soon.'

'Oh yes, I'll be back for more.'

When he'd gone, Brooke said right away, 'Let's open the Champagne, Truly.'

'Yes, we deserve a drink. Oh by the way, where's Judy? She should have been here by now.'

'She's probably too stoned to get out of bed.'

'Say again?'

'Couldn't you tell, Truly? She's a druggie.'

'You're joking?'

'No, I'm not. Besides, she told me she was going to get a fix as soon as she'd earned okay.'

'If that's the case, I'm going to have to get rid of her.'

'Wait till you have somebody else first.'

'I suppose so, but in the meantime I'm going to have words with her.'

After swigging back the Champagne on empty stomachs we soon got a bit pissed, so I suggested we have a rest. Brooke went to lie on the bed and I settled myself on the sofa. When I woke up it was dark outside. I could hardly believe it, I'd slept for three hours and not one missed call. I'd noticed a steady decline in the number of calls since just after Christmas and had put it down to the fact that most people were short of cash at the beginning of the year. I only hoped things would pick up soon.

Savannah hadn't been too happy on her first Wednesday in the New Year. She only managed to get one punter all day, and said if it was going to be the same next week she'd have to stop working here as it wasn't worth it.

What I couldn't understand was I now had a few lovely girls, we'd dropped the sexual service prices and I had several ads in the paper as well as Internet advertising, so why wasn't business getting better? I didn't know what else to do, other than change location. I told myself I should be happy, as the flat was making a small profit every week, but the truth was I was bored running a small town knocking-shop.

The decision to close the flat came sooner rather than later. I received a voicemail on one of the sex phones a few weeks later as I was getting ready to go to work. I thought it would be Judy telling me she was unable to come in again today. Brooke had been right about her, she did have a habit, but I kept her on because I felt sorry for her.

As I listened to the voicemail my heart began to race. A very well-spoken lady, claiming to be from the Residents' Association, had left a polite but threatening message: 'It has been brought to our attention that number 49 _____ Street is operating as a brothel. This is an illegal act and will not be tolerated in this town. The police, and the council, have been informed and the appropriate action will be taken to close you down.'

The first thing I did, as always in a crisis, was to phone my solicitor. After relaying what the woman had said, word for word, Andrew suspected it could be a hoax, possibly from another brothel just wanting to get rid of the competition, or perhaps I'd upset a punter in some way.

I immediately remembered having words with a particularly unsavoury punter Brooke had had the misfortune of having to shag a couple of weeks before. When I took the call he said he had a very high sex drive, and wanted a full personal and O without. After being in the bedroom for a few minutes Brooke came out and told me his dick was scabby and there was no way she was going to suck it without a condom. I told her to tell him it would have to be oral with or nothing at all, and if he had any problems he could talk to me.

A couple of days later he rang again and asked for someone else to perform O without. I politely told him that if he visited a doctor and got his dick treated, then he could come back and see us. If not, he wasn't welcome. Understandably, he didn't react too well to what I'd said. He retaliated by saying I was just a fucking prostitute who now ran a whorehouse, and instead of making money from girls opening their legs why didn't I get a proper job. I remained calm and told him not to call again.

When I asked Andrew why he thought it was a hoax, he told me he didn't think the Residents' Association would contact me by phone. That wouldn't be how they'd play it; a letter was more appropriate. We both agreed that whoever it was, they could and probably would make trouble for me. It was just a question of time before they notified the police and council, if they hadn't already.

Andrew repeated what he'd said after Beulah tried to bring me down. When you offer sexual services you're very vulnerable in every way, not only from psychotic punters but competitors, dissatisfied punters and neighbours who suspect you. He advised me to look for new premises before the police got involved. When he suggested a certain town, I asked why he thought it would be good. He told me he was the Duty Solicitor there, and in all the years he'd attended the station it was never for anything to do with prostitution or running brothels. Apparently, the police there had a relaxed attitude towards knocking-shops, and as long as they didn't cause any problems in the neighbourhood they turned a blind eye. I told Andrew I'd give it serious consideration and keep him informed of what was going on.

I was sure the town Andrew suggested was good. The problem was I'd set my sights higher, and somehow the idea of setting up a knocking-shop there didn't quite live up to my expectations.

I was convinced that London was the place to make good money and fast. All I needed to do was find a way to rent premises. I knew of only one and that was to contact a man Beulah had introduced me to a few years before.

Chapter 22

At that time my partner and I had a six-month separation and I spent a lot of time with Beulah. She wanted to introduce me to a friend of hers who owned an estate agency business based on Edgware Road, London. She said he would be good for me, as he was loaded and could afford to spoil me.

I wasn't too keen on the idea, but Beulah managed to talk me into accompanying her the next time she had to see Marvin. A few days later she rang and said she'd arranged a luncheon meeting for the next day.

'I hope you haven't said anything embarrassing, Beulah.'

'Don't be stupid, I've just asked if it's okay to bring my friend.'

'Are you sure that's all, cos I know how big your mouth can be?'

'I promise I've said nothing about you.'

'Okay then, what time shall I get to yours?'

'Make it eleven, and then we can jump on the train to London.'

As I got ready the next morning I couldn't help thinking how silly this was. I didn't know anything about Marvin, and knowing Beulah he most certainly already knew far too much about my life. I didn't feel ready to go out with anyone yet, as I was still crying myself to sleep every night over splitting up with my partner and had the bags under my eyes to prove it. I assured myself Marvin would take one look at me and wonder what on earth Beulah was thinking.

On the short walk from Marble Arch tube station to Edgware Road, Beulah told me how she'd met Marvin. She'd bought her Spanish apartment from him a couple of years back in the days before she got into financial difficulties, and he also managed a flat she let out in London. Meeting Marvin today was not only for my benefit. Beulah was going to ask him to sell both the apartment in Spain and the London flat before they were repossessed.

'What makes you think he's going to be interested in me?'

'He's desperate for a bit of TLC. He told me the last time I saw him.'

We arrived at Marvin's shop, and while Beulah smoked a cigarette I contemplated doing a runner. I think she sensed what I was thinking, because she stubbed half her cigarette out and before I could escape she grabbed my arm and yanked me through the door. We were greeted by a very handsome Arabian-looking man of about thirty-five.

'Hello, Sami, where's Marvin?'

'He's in his office. He's expecting you.'

I followed Beulah as she marched towards the back of the shop and banged on a half-glazed frosted door.

A man shouted, 'Come in, ladies.'

He had the face and body of an old bloated toad, bulging watery eyes and a huge, almost lipless mouth. His belly was so swollen it looked as though it would pop if poked with a pin. Altogether he was very unfortunate looking. As Beulah kissed Marvin hello, I couldn't help grinning and thinking there wasn't much chance of him turning into a prince.

Beulah then introduced me, and as he leant forward to kiss me I put my hand towards him and we shook hands instead. After the necessary introductions were out of the way and coffee had been brought in by a member of Marvin's staff, we sat around his desk, and for the next hour he talked non-stop. His favourite subject seemed to be himself. He delighted in telling us how successful he was and what he'd achieved in his life. As I sat there trying to suppress the urge to yawn, I couldn't help thinking how Beulah could possibly think I'd be interested in this obnoxious man. Not only was he hideously ugly but also extremely boring. Finally Beulah and Marvin talked about her properties, and after another coffee she was ready to leave.

Just when I thought I'd escaped Beulah's matchmaking, she said, 'Why don't you take her out one evening? She could do with cheering up.'

Without hesitation Marvin looked at me excitedly and replied, 'Oh, I'd love to.'

I don't know if it was embarrassment or the sudden urge to escape that made me agree to dinner, but I knew it was too late to back out because Beulah gave Marvin my telephone number.

I waited until we were a safe distance from his shop before saying, 'I couldn't possibly have that unfortunate-looking man, not even if you served him up boiled, baked, battered or fried.'

She looked at me and laughed. 'Don't be silly, you don't have to eat him, just fuck him a few times and he'll be putty in your hands.'

'I don't think I could. He's far too revolting.'

'I would if I were in your position. At least he can afford to spoil you.'

'I thought he was taking us to lunch?'

'So did I. Maybe he was too busy.'

It didn't take long for Marvin to make contact. The following afternoon he rang and for the next forty-five minutes spoke about the problems he was having with his mother. She'd recently been diagnosed with Alzheimer's, and he had to sort out carers for her. I listened attentively and tried to say the right things when I managed to get a word in. Eventually he got round to the real reason for phoning me.

'Would you care to join me for dinner on Friday night, in London at about eight o'clock?'

I found myself saying yes and we arranged to meet at his shop at seven thirty.

After looking through my wardrobe for several minutes I chose my little black Karen Millen wool crêpe dress. It was classically designed, sleeveless, round neck and cut low enough to reveal a little cleavage, with the hem just above the knee. This dress had stood me in good stead at many a party, wedding and the occasional funeral over the years.

I drove to Bromley South Station, as the trains would be more frequent for my journey back home. The train was rather full and there were several young couples who were obviously in love, kissing and caressing each other completely unaware of anyone else. What could I expect? It was Friday night and people were out to enjoy themselves.

My mind drifted back to the first time I met my partner. I was out for the evening with a couple of girlfriends. We walked into a pub and made our way to the bar when I spotted an extremely good-looking man. He had beautiful large blue eyes and gypsy features. His hair was mousey-blonde and long enough to be tied back in the same way as David Beckham at the time. The attraction felt so strong I knew I had to have him, despite both my friends warning me that he looked rough. By the end of the evening I was hopelessly in love.

My thoughts were interrupted by a strong Birmingham accent on the Tannoy announcing that the train was pulling into Victoria Station. I made my way to the underground and caught the tube to Marble Arch. Then I made the short walk to Edgware Road. I stopped briefly in a shop doorway, pulled a compact mirror out of my handbag and checked my make-up. *You'll do*, I thought. After all, the guy I was about to meet was no oil painting. Just then the heavens opened and I had to run the couple of blocks to Marvin's shop in order to avoid arriving looking like a drowned rat.

I stepped in the door just as Marvin was in the middle of some kind of business deal with two Arabian gentlemen. They looked on in amazement as Marvin made a lunge for me, and before I knew what was happening he'd clamped his mouth over mine and suddenly I was gasping for air. It felt as though I had a plumber's plunger over my mouth. After a few seconds he unclamped his slobbery lips. He then composed himself and introduced me to the two gentlemen as his girlfriend. I couldn't help feeling embarrassed, not only by the show of affection in front of the men but also his announcement.

The rest of the evening was similar to the first time I'd met Marvin. He talked non-stop about himself. The only compensation was his good taste in restaurants and the meal was great. At the end of the evening, after managing to avoid another slobbering from his lips, I pecked him on the cheek and promised to stay in touch.

I had no intention of contacting him again, and after a few days of no news I suspected he'd got the message. I was taken by surprise that afternoon when the doorbell rang and Interflora delivered a large bouquet of flowers. The card read *I'm besotted by you. Marvin*. Perhaps Beulah was right. Marvin had money to spoil me so I may as well take advantage of it. He'd given me his telephone number so I decided to give him a call and thank him for the flowers. As I dialled the number I remembered something amusing an old boyfriend used to say. If you have sex with an ugly person put a paper bag over their head, and one on yours in case theirs blows off. It was said in jest, but in Marvin's case it may be necessary. I endured a couple more boring dates before the inevitable nearly took place.

Marvin booked a table at one of his favourite restaurants and a room at the Hilton hotel. When I asked why the hotel, he gave the unconvincing reply that he only had my safety in mind and didn't like the idea of me having to travel late at night, so I reluctantly agreed. It was arranged that I was to check into the hotel for a drink prior to going for dinner. Marvin was waiting in the reception area when I arrived.

'Sorry I'm late. Have you been waiting long?'

'A couple of hours, but it's okay, it gave me time to unwind.'

Yuk, I thought, *there's nothing more unattractive than a desperate man, and this one must have been waiting with his dick in his hand.*

The porter took my bag and showed us up to the room. As soon as he closed the door Marvin was all over me. I could smell his whisky breath as he caressed my neck and shoulders, and for a moment I wondered what the hell I was doing. It felt wrong. I'd always believed desire comes before sex and I didn't even like this man.

I noticed a bottle of Champagne cooling in an ice bucket on the bedside cabinet and asked him for a glass. He poured a couple of glasses, and after drinking his he noticed the time.

'We need to hurry if we want to eat out, or would you rather we eat in the room?'

Without replying, I put my coat on, grabbed my bag and moved towards the door.

During the meal Marvin waffled on happily as I pretended to be interested in what he had to say. The truth was my mind was somewhere else. Apart from a few meals and a bunch of flowers Marvin was hardly the sugar daddy I was hoping for. I'd once had an affair with an older man who, after only three weeks of dating and one night of sex, bought me an E-type Jaguar. Now that man had style. Towards the end of the meal I noticed Marvin kept checking the time.

'Is everything okay, Marvin?'

'I'm sorry, I won't be able to stay all night. I've got to get back in case my mother needs me.'

What a relief, I thought, *I won't have to endure him for too much longer.*

'I'd like to see you back to your room before making my way home. Is that okay?'

'Yes, of course Marvin, but I warn you, I'm a little tired.'

'Oh, I'm sure I can wake you up.'

I very much doubted that. He was the reason for my lethargy and had virtually bored me to sleep.

Back at the room Marvin made himself comfortable on the bed while I used the bathroom. As I stood looking in the mirror I contemplated the best course of action. I felt entirely responsible for the position I was in as I had encouraged the man. I couldn't very well act like a silly teenager by saying I wasn't sure if I wanted sex. The best course of action was to fuck him and then fuck him off.

I stripped down to my bra and knickers, kept on my high-heeled stilettos and walked out of the bathroom. As I walked towards the bed I unclipped my bra and began to fondle my nipples. Marvin lay silently as I stood in front of him playing with my breasts, and after a few seconds he put his hand down his trousers and began to play with himself. While he lay wanking himself, I took out a condom I'd bought earlier from the machine in the restaurant. As soon as I lay on the bed Marvin stripped off his clothes.

I noticed his dick wasn't hard and he said, 'I'm sorry, but my dick doesn't get as hard as I'd like these days.'

Oh shit, I thought. I'd suffered this boring old man all evening, the least he could do was give me a good seeing to.

'But I can please you with my tongue.'

Marvin would have got ten out of ten if he was in a competition, but no matter how hard he tried I couldn't come. After quite some time I faked an orgasm to put him out of his misery. It was bad enough for him to have a dick that didn't work, so the least I could do was make him feel he'd satisfied me in other ways.

'Let me suck your cock now.'

I managed to roll the condom on his soft dick and then sucked it for so long I felt I'd developed lockjaw. Thankfully, he came just as I was about to give up. I left Marvin to get dressed while I popped into the bathroom. After a few minutes he tapped on the door.

'I'm sorry, I have to go now, but I'll pop back in the morning for a cuddle before I go to work.'

'But I'll be leaving straight after breakfast.'

'Don't worry, I'll be here to join you for breakfast in bed.'

Oh no, I thought. I didn't think I could stomach another helping of his cock. I opened the door a little. 'Okay, Marvin, see you in the morning.'

He caught me by surprise with another of those slobbery kisses. Just as he was about to leave, he said, 'If you want anything to drink, just put it on the room and I'll pay for it in the morning.'

'Thank you, Marvin.'

As soon as he left I ran a bath. I felt dirty and disgusted with myself.

I woke up the next morning with a thumping headache and remembered Marvin was going to call in for breakfast. I leapt out of bed to wash and dress; I needed to move fast if I didn't want his little sausage for breakfast. I'd just finished when there was a knock on the door, and when I opened it I was unable to avoid his kiss and cuddle. He pinned me up against the bathroom door and for a few moments I suffered as he groped and slobbered me.

Thankfully, just as he whispered in my ear, 'Let's go to bed,' my mobile rang.

'Do you have to answer that?'

'I'm sorry, Marvin.'

I pulled away from him and answered the phone. My mother rarely rang me, let alone to ask for my help, so the call and timing was nothing short of a miracle. Marvin was bitterly disappointed as I explained mother couldn't babysit my niece because of a hospital appointment, so I was needed to take her place.

Chapter 23

I didn't date Marvin again but we stayed in touch by phone, and the last time we spoke I told him all about Beulah and what she'd done to me. He wasn't surprised and went on to tell me how she and her husband had caused a big fight in the shop a couple of months before. They blamed him for their financial ruin because he didn't always manage to find tenants for her London flat, so for several weeks it stood empty. She'd also bought the Spanish apartment through Marvin's agency, and accused him of asking too much for it. When Marvin tried to explain that the property market had its ups and downs, she went crazy and threatened to smash the shop up unless he gave her some money back. He gave them a small amount just to get rid of them.

I decided it was best to come clean with Marvin and tell him exactly what I wanted the flat for. He answered the phone and immediately recognised my voice, even though we hadn't spoken for some time. He didn't bat an eyelid when I told him I wanted to open a brothel in London. He said he had a few easy-going landlords that were happy for their flats to be used as discreet knocking-shops, as long as the neighbours were respected and it wasn't operated twenty-four hours a day. He then put me on hold for a few minutes while he transferred me to Raymond, who was a member of his team that dealt with lettings. Raymond described a flat that was currently available, just off Tottenham Court Road in the Fitzrovia area.

He thought the flat was ideal because it was on a monthly contract, so if I wanted to leave for any reason I only needed to give a month's notice. The rent was a bit expensive at five hundred and fifty pounds a week, but as Raymond pointed out, other than the telephone, all bills were included in the price. I agreed to meet him outside the property the next day at one o'clock. I then rang Brooke and asked her to come with me to view the flat. I wanted a second opinion and hers was important, as she had experience of other flats in the London area.

We chatted excitedly on the journey up at the prospect of having a flat in such an affluent part of London. Brooke said she'd worked in a flat in the Oxford Street area that had a constant flow of punters calling from the cards they'd put in the telephone boxes. I knew nothing about cards in telephone boxes or how they worked. I thought surely there was no need to advertise in this way with so many men having access to a computer. Telephone box advertising seemed very seedy and must attract undesirables. I needed to give Savannah a ring when I got home and pick her brains, as she'd also worked in London. It would be good to hear what she knew on the subject.

The flat was one of a block of sixteen and situated on the third floor. The entrance lobby and lift had a luxurious look, with black marble floor and mirrored walls. The main door was fitted with an entry phone system and CCTV, which was reassuring in case we had any unsavoury characters at the door. The flat had a reasonable-sized bedroom and an open-plan sitting room and kitchen, but the bathroom and hallway were very small.

If the flat was to make a profit, I needed to have two girls working each day, and that meant putting a bed in the sitting room. The only problem was, if both girls had a punter at the same time I had nowhere to go. I couldn't very well sit in the kitchen, because it was open to the sitting room, so the only option was the hallway, but it was too small for a chair. I then thought of the fisherman's seat at home that I used in the garden, as it was very comfortable. It would be perfect and could quickly be folded up and put out of the way.

The flat was furnished and even had a flat-screen TV with Sky. That would be good to entertain the girls during the dull moments, which hopefully wouldn't be very often. I had two issues about the flat. The first was that there were three neighbours on my floor, and even more above and below. When I told Raymond of this concern he said it shouldn't be a problem. Most of the flats were let out to people on a short-term basis and quite a few were used by Japanese businessmen and so were empty most of the time. My other worry was the address. I wondered if punters would remember the name of the road, the name and number of the block of flats, and the number of the flat itself. Probably not. Experience had taught me that men seemed incapable of remembering the simplest of instructions when they were thinking about their dicks, and it wasn't unusual for a punter to ring two or three times because he'd forgotten the address.

After having another look around the flat, I thanked Raymond and said I needed time to think about it. Brooke loved the flat and thought it would make an ideal first-time place. She agreed with me about the address, but because it was on a monthly basis we could just use it for a short period. When we had enough regular punters we could look for a better place in the same area.

After giving it serious consideration over the next few days, I rang Raymond to tell him I'd like to take the flat at the end of the month. This only gave me a couple of weeks and I had so much to do. I needed to advertise in the London area for staff and as Brooke and Savannah had told me, that meant an ad in the Loot, as that's where all the girls looked for work in Central London. I intended to advertise the business as an escort agency under various different directory listings on the Internet, so I also needed to have a website designed.

A week after placing the ad in the Loot the girls started calling. I'd planned on interviewing as many as possible over the course of two days, and after taking a name and brief description, I gave them the address, date and time of the interview. Apart from a couple of girls wanting to do a working interview, the rest were quite happy to come along for a formal interview on the understanding that they may not get the job.

The day of picking up the keys finally arrived. After transferring four thousand two hundred pounds for the deposit and one month's rent into Marvin's business account, Raymond met me at the flat to hand them over.

As I walked along Tottenham Court Road on my way home I couldn't help looking in the telephone boxes. I felt a sudden rush of anxiety. Maybe I was out of my depth here. After all, I knew very little about the London scene. What if I encountered dangerous people? I couldn't very well go to the police. I hadn't even checked out the competition and where they were situated. What if they decided to make my life difficult? By the time I'd reached the underground I felt sick with nerves, so I went into a café for a cup of tea before going any further. After a few sips I began to calm down. This was going to be a new chapter in my life, and even though I was scared I could see that London had the potential to make me a lot more money than a sleepy little town in Kent. Tottenham Court Road alone was swarming with prosperous-looking businessmen of all shapes and sizes.

When I got home my partner had some good news. My uncle had rung to say he'd taken on a rather large building contract, and if my partner could help him he'd pay him six hundred a week. This was great news. Not only because we'd be financially better off, but it also meant my partner wouldn't have the time to interfere with my business.

With the website ready the evening before the interview day, I decided to give the girls a ring to find out if they were happy to participate in a photo shoot. As I expected they were okay about it, as long as their faces were not going to appear on the Internet. I promised them no facial shots would be taken, and only after their approval would I put them on the Internet.

Glamour photography was not my forte, and so as the father of my children was a photographer I asked him to do the job. We'd split up years ago but remained very close friends. He knew all about what I'd been up to in order to survive, and even though he was extremely pissed off with my partner he didn't stand in judgment. What did sadden him was that even though he was an internationally known photographer, like many artists he was usually broke and could rarely help me out financially. Paul was delighted at the prospect of having to photograph beautiful young ladies and promised to meet me at the flat at noon on the interview day.

Later that evening I sent a text to Brooke to let her know what was happening. She was getting desperate to start working because, as usual, she was skint. Her husband worked full time and managed to cover the rent each month, but it was up to her to pay the household bills. The problem was she had expensive taste in clothes and shoes along with a shopping addiction. It was not unusual for her to pop out for lunch only to return with two or three pairs of shoes with matching handbags and several items of clothing. I've never been particularly interested in traipsing around shops looking for clothes and only shop when I absolutely have to. But I couldn't help admiring Brooke; she always looked stunning.

I received a text back asking if I wanted her help with the interviews. Up until now Brooke had proved to be a good judge of character when it came to girls and punters, so I thought having her at the interviews would be beneficial. I texted back yes and the time of the train I was taking up to London.

Shortly after we got to the flat, Paul arrived. He had a look around and suggested we move a large chest of drawers out of the bedroom because it was a bit cluttered for a photo shoot. We had just managed to move it when the entry phone buzzer rang.

After eight hours we had interviewed twelve girls and Paul had photographed ten of them. One girl declined due to not having any sexy underwear on, and the other girl flatly refused to be photographed by Paul. I doubted the experience she claimed to have had, because normally girls who have worked in the sex industry for a while don't mind taking their clothes off, especially if it's going to increase their chances of earning money. I respected her wishes though and told her I may still be able to offer her work in the flat instead of escort work.

When the last girl had left we sat and discussed all of the girls. In my opinion there was only one I wasn't prepared to take on the books and Brooke agreed with me. It wasn't because there was anything wrong with her, but she came to the interview with someone I can only describe as her lesbian pimp. She didn't tell me she was bringing anyone with her to the interview, so when I opened the door and was faced with a pretty young lady and an obese, ugly woman of about thirty-five with facial hair, I was taken completely by surprise. When I politely asked about her, the fat woman said, 'I'm her girlfriend!' Before I had a chance to reply they walked right past me through to the sitting room, where they plonked themselves down on the sofa. Paul looked at me and I could see he was stifling a grin. After trying to ask the pretty girl a couple of questions about herself, it quickly became apparent that her ugly girlfriend wore the trousers because she answered all the questions for her. The poor pretty girl didn't have a chance to move her lips. I couldn't help thinking the scene reminded me of a ventriloquist's dummy that had taken over its operator.

After another day of interviewing and a total of twenty profiles on the website, I was confident we were going to be busy from the first day. With two different girls available to work at the flat each day and a lovely selection on the website for escort duties, I opened for business.

Chapter 24

For the next three weeks I worked hard trying to get the escort agency and the flat up and running. The response from the website and the ad in the Loot was dreadful. There was no shortage of girls ringing for work, but the punters were few and far between. Even more frustrating was to lose the odd rare punter who rang wanting an outcall with a girl he fancied on the website. When I contacted her to tell her she had a booking, she was either busy doing something else or simply not answering her phone.

The problem was I didn't have enough work to give them. I should have realised the competition in London would be fierce, and I was just a tiny fish in a huge ocean. I didn't even have enough calls coming in to warrant opening the flat, so for the time being it remained closed. Brooke became so desperate during that time that she started working a couple of days a week at a flat in Liverpool Street. It felt like desertion, but I knew I'd have done the same thing in her shoes, and she didn't mean anything personal by leaving. It was just a matter of survival.

I was beginning to think Savannah had been right. When I told her I'd taken a flat in London she thought I was crazy, especially as I had no experience of the place. When I told her I'd advertised on the Internet she said I couldn't possibly survive, unless I used minicab drivers or put cards in telephone boxes.

To do that I'd need to hire a card man. When I said I could do it myself to save money, she laughed and said, 'If you do, you'll end up in prison.'

'Then what's the thing with the minicab drivers?'

'You have to talk to the drivers that sit outside nightclubs and do a deal with them. Generally, they take fifty per cent of what you charge the punter, so you charge three hundred and give the driver one fifty.'

'But most punters aren't prepared to pay that kind of money.'

'Rich drunk ones are.'

Up until then I'd laid out over six thousand pounds and was getting desperate to claw some money back. The problem I faced was how to go about promoting a knocking-shop without attracting the wrong kind of attention. I couldn't very well hand out leaflets.

One of the reasons Brooke and I liked the flat so much was because it was within spitting distance of a famous gentlemen's strip club where Brooke had once worked. She reckoned the club was merely somewhere the men got teased and frustrated, so if they knew about us they could pop along and get relieved. I figured what I needed was someone on the inside who could discreetly send the punters in my direction, and in return receive a small cut. The few times I'd walked past the club a particular middle-aged doorman always winked and said hello. Maybe he was the man for the job.

The following day I caught the train to London and waited in a café opposite the club. After a little more than an hour, the middle-aged doorman appeared and took up his position outside the entrance to the club. I wanted to appear completely natural, as if I was just walking past the club, so I walked a bit further along Tottenham Court Road towards Goodge Street. Once out of sight, I crossed the road and walked back to the club.

With increasing trepidation, I approached the club and as I got nearer my man caught sight of me. I smiled, and thankfully he spoke.

'Hello, darling, how are you today?'

'I'm very well, thanks.'

'I've seen you a few times. Do you work around here?'

What a result! He was right on cue, and here was my opening.

'As a matter of fact, I do.'

'Whereabouts?'

'Just round the corner.'

'Are you a doctor from the hospital?'

I looked at him and grinned. 'No, but I do offer a kind of treatment.'

Judging by the quizzical look he gave me I knew he was curious and dying to know more.

'Why don't you take me for a coffee and I'll tell you what I do?'

Over a cappuccino, I put my proposition to John. After listening to what I had to offer, he said he'd love to earn some extra cash. The problem was most of the girls that stripped at the club were on the game, and they used the place as a way to pick up more punters. Even though the club had strict rules forbidding prostitution, it still went on. The girls simply gave their mobile numbers to customers that showed an interest in them. An arrangement would then usually be made to meet up at a local hotel when the girl's shift ended.

John agreed to send punters to me whenever possible, and in return he would receive fifty pounds. I then gave him my number, thanked him for his time and left. As I made my way home I couldn't help thinking the meeting had been a complete waste of time. I certainly wasn't going to hold my breath waiting for punters from John's direction. After all, blokes that had already had a taste of a chocolate box selection of girls were more likely to choose one of them, if on offer, rather than risk visiting a knocking-shop.

Out of sheer desperation I then did a crazy thing that could have turned out very nasty. One of the girls I'd interviewed mentioned she had a contact that might be useful to me, especially as I'd just opened up and could use some help. The contact was an African man who ran a minicab business and often supplied knocking-shops with punters. At the time of the interview I didn't think I'd need such help and had declined to take his number.

After an evening of mulling things over, I made the call. Mellissa was pleased to hear from me and keen to know what had been going on since the interview. She wasn't surprised when I told her I hadn't managed to get the flat going and so needed all the help I could get.

The name of her contact was Joe, and after giving me his number she said, 'Make sure you tell him I gave you his number or he won't talk to you. He'll think you're the police.'

I thanked her and said I'd get in touch when I had some work.

Joe was reluctant to talk at first. After I answered his questions as to who I was, where I was and how I'd got his number, he seemed satisfied that I wasn't a threat and agreed to do business. He told me I'd need a credit card machine for punters that didn't have cash, and he wanted a hundred business cards with my telephone number to hand out to his drivers. I arranged to meet him outside Grove Park Station in south-east London at eight the following night with the cards.

When I put the phone down I immediately felt uneasy about using Joe. I just didn't like the sound of him. He was too smooth. It also bothered me about the credit card machine as I'd never needed one before and it seemed very risky. If the police raided, it would provide a traceable record.

I wanted Joe to know I had a man on the scene, so I told my partner what I was doing and asked him to accompany me to Grove Park. He wasn't happy about me involving a complete stranger, and said, 'For all you know he's probably a pimp, and a dangerous one if you get on the wrong side of him.' But after explaining to him that I was only going to use him for a little while until things picked up, he reluctantly agreed to go with me.

Before going to bed we printed two hundred cards on the PC using a picture of a bikini-clad girl lying over a Bugatti Veyron, along with a different mobile number from the website and paper so that I could instantly recognise where the call was coming from. The quality wasn't brilliant, but they were good enough.

The following evening we arrived at a quarter to eight outside Grove Park Station. My partner insisted we park the car discreetly and watch from a safe distance. When I asked why, he said, 'Don't you understand the business you're doing is dangerous? It's good to take precautions!'

'What precautions?'

'We don't want him to know anything about us.'

'But how's he going to find out if we don't tell him?'

'If he sees our number plate he can find out where we live.'

My partner had a very untrusting nature that I didn't always agree with, but in this situation he was right to be wary. After all, we knew nothing about the man we were about to meet, or what part he wanted in my business. Until we knew more, it was wise to play safe.

After sitting for quite some time, and feeling sick from my partner's endless smoking, I noticed a black Mercedes with tinted windows pulling up outside the station.

'Do you think that's him?'

'Maybe, but let's wait a bit to see if he gets out.' After smoking another cigarette, he said, 'Come on, I don't want to sit here all night. Let's go see if it's him.'

I felt very vulnerable as we stood outside the station, knowing the driver could observe us from behind the tinted windows without giving away his own identity. Just as we were beginning to think that the Mercedes driver wasn't Joe, the front passenger window opened and the driver leant across.

'Are you, Truly?' he asked.

I replied a little hesitantly, 'Yes, I am, and this is my partner.'

'Get in so we can talk.'

My partner pushed me slightly, opened the back door and we climbed in.

I was startled by Joe's immense frame. His shoulders were so broad they overflowed onto the driver's door and passenger seat and his head touched the roof. I don't know how he managed to get in and out of the vehicle let alone drive it with his enormous chest rubbing against the steering wheel.

As soon as my partner closed the door Joe turned his head round and smiled, flashing a mouthful of gold teeth at us. After the introductions, Joe told us he ran an upmarket minicab business which used prestige cars with uniformed drivers for hotel, nightclub and airport runs. It was an established business and he had many wealthy clients on his books, most of them men.

The other side to Joe's business involved prostitution. Not only did he take punters to flats, he also had several girls working for him who visited punters at their own homes or hotels.

When I asked him why he didn't have his own flat instead of taking punters to other flats, he laughed, saying, 'Why should I risk getting caught by the police when there're ladies, like you, willing to do that?'

I ignored his comment, and he proceeded to explain how we were going to work together. Whenever a punter wanted to visit my flat I would receive a phone call from Joe letting me know what time the driver and punter were due to arrive. If, at any time, a driver rang or brought a punter without Joe calling first, I was to inform him immediately, because it meant the driver was trying to rip him off.

Then he said, 'If I find out you kept quiet about this then I'll take action to get my cut.'

I was right to be wary of Joe. He didn't directly threaten me, but I understood what he meant. A credit card machine, along with alcoholic drinks on offer, was an absolute must to encourage punters to spend more time and money. When I told him I didn't like the idea of serving alcohol to punters in case they got abusive, he laughed and said, 'That's no problem. The driver will be with you.'

'But what can he do if he's on another job?'

'Didn't I tell you? The driver stays in the flat for as long as the punter. That's so I know how much you owe me, cos in the past some ladies have tried ripping me off by saying the punter only stayed for half an hour, or he changed his mind and left without having a girl.'

'What percentage do I have to pay you?'

'I want fifty per cent, so you have to charge the punter three hundred quid an hour.'

'How do I pay you if the punter has paid with a credit card?'

'It's your job to make sure you've got enough cash at the flat to pay the driver.'

'But that's not always possible, especially at night. Can't I pay into an account of yours the next day?'

'No. You have to pay the driver that night or else I'll have to come and see you.' As he looked round and flashed his gold teeth at me again, I wondered how many women he had threatened in order to be able to afford those gnashers. 'But don't worry, Truly, as long as you pay what's owed we'll get along great, you'll see.'

Little did he realise that I'd already heard and seen enough, and judging by my partner's silence throughout the meeting he was on the same wavelength.

I then handed over the cards, knowing I had no intention of doing business with this pimp. I only hoped this was going to be our first, and last, meeting. We shook hands and he promised to call me the following evening. We got out of the car and my partner directed me to a takeaway across the road so we could wait until Joe drove away.

My partner waited until we were on our way home before he gave his opinion of Joe. He thought he was an extremely nasty piece of work and that I'd be crazy to allow him to get involved in the business. I should also forget the idea of using him for a short period of time until the business picked up, because once you let that kind of person in you'd never be able to shake him off. He's far too greedy. It would be a much better idea to put cards in telephone boxes and risk getting caught by the police than risk your safety by using that scum.

Fortunately, I hadn't given Joe the address of the flat. He only knew it was in the Fitzrovia area. He also had no idea where we lived, so all I had to do was destroy the SIM card and hope I never ran into that character again.

Chapter 25

Alfter spending a sleepless night worrying and still having no answers to my predicament (by the morning I was almost ready to give up and hand the keys back), Paul came to my rescue. When I rang and told him what had been happening, or more to the point not happening, he offered to put cards in telephone boxes until I found a proper card man. He said he knew it was now illegal, but if it helped me out he was willing to take the risk.

I wasn't happy about having to put him at risk, but after much deliberation I decided to accept his offer. So that evening my partner and I printed some more cards, using the same picture as before but with a different mobile number.

Paul didn't let me down. As promised, he was waiting for me outside Goodge Street Station.

When I asked him how long he had been waiting he replied, 'I got here early so I could walk around and count the telephone boxes in the area.'

'Why?'

'So I know how many cards I'll need, and which side streets have boxes.'

After a cup of tea Paul was ready to make a start. As I handed him the cards he asked, 'What are you going to do when the phone rings?'

'You mean if it rings.'

'Don't be negative. It's going to ring, so I suggest you give the Romanian girl a call. The one that wouldn't take her clothes off.'

'Why her? I thought she was bullshitting at the interview.'

'I thought she was a peach, even without make-up.'

'But I really didn't think she was serious about working.'

'Just give her a ring, and if she's not willing you'll have to find somebody else, and bloody quick before the phone starts ringing. I'd better get going cos I wanna finish carding up by lunchtime.'

'Please be careful.'

'No worries. I'll be back at the flat when I've finished.'

A few minutes after Paul left I looked through my diary and found the girl's number. Alice was surprised when I called her because a month had gone by since her interview. I explained that up until now I hadn't had one punter through the door, and I wasn't sure if the cards being put out as we were speaking would generate any business.

She then surprised me by saying, 'I don't mind waiting at the flat until things start happening.'

'But it may take some time, Alice.'

'That's okay, I understand. Anyway, I'm going to make my way to the flat now, okay?'

'Thank you, Alice. See you soon.'

When I put the phone down I couldn't believe how understanding she had been. Maybe it was because she was new to the work and hadn't become hard yet. While waiting for Alice to arrive I made a cup of tea and put the television on. It had been almost an hour since Paul left and so far no calls. I began to worry that he'd been caught already; just our luck to get nicked before we had a punter through the door.

My thoughts were interrupted when the sex phone started ringing, but I didn't know where I'd left it. Shit! *The first call and I'm going to miss it*, I thought. I rushed to the bathroom where the sound of ringing was coming from, when it stopped. *Oh fuck, how stupid am I?* The phone was on top of the cistern. I must have left it there when I went to the loo. I looked at the missed call and didn't recognise the number so assumed it must have been a punter. I was overwhelmed with a mixture of emotions and didn't know whether to laugh or cry. I told myself not to worry, it would ring again, and just then the entry phone buzzer rang. It was Alice, so I buzzed her in and went to the door. Paul was right, she was very beautiful: her eyes were bright blue and her long, dark hair and luscious large lips complemented her flawless milky complexion.

'Hi, Alice, it's good to see you.'

'How're things, Truly? Has the phone rung?'

'Yes, once, but I stupidly missed it.'

'It'll ring again. You'll see.'

Alice got comfy on the sofa and began applying some make-up. While I was getting coffee and cookies ready the phone rang and this time I was ready for it. As I started to give the punter details it was obvious he was in a hurry because he wasn't interested. He just wanted the address. When I tried to explain that he needed to know the rates he butted in.

'Look, love, I'm on my lunch break and I don't have much time. Anyway, I know the going rate in the area, so if you give me the address I'll be around soon.'

I didn't want to lose a punter and sound difficult in front of Alice, so I just gave him the address.

Alice didn't need to be told what to do. She was already stripping off, and after putting on a sexy bra and knickers she pulled on a little black silky low-cut dress.

'How do I look, Truly?'

'You look fantastic. I love the dress.'

'Yes, it's my favourite.'

She then went on to explain that the other place she worked at insisted every girl wore a sexy black dress because gentlemen with money liked the girls to look classy. When I asked where the flat was she said it was in Shepherd Market and was run by a crazy Italian lady called Rosy. She tried to run an upmarket knocking-shop and charged two hundred and fifty to three hundred pounds an hour. The flat had four bedrooms and was opulently furnished with heavy silk and velvet drapes, and all the rooms had antique furniture with ornate gilt mirrors.

Rosy had strict rules, one being that the girls had to give every punter an oil massage for a full thirty minutes prior to doing anything sexual. At the end of the session she insisted on talking to the punter to find out what he thought of the service and the girl's performance. Alice said most of the punters were reluctant to talk, but Rosy was so persistent they often had little choice.

Rosy still offered herself for sexual services, although Alice reckoned she was well into her fifties. Her husband worked at the flat as a general dogsbody, emptying the condom bins and cleaning the rooms at the end of each day. I laughed and said I couldn't imagine my partner doing that.

I was relieved when Alice told me that when she began working there the flat had only been open for two months, and like me Rosy didn't have a card man so her husband did the job. I was glad to hear I wasn't the only complete amateur to open a brothel.

We both jumped when the entry buzzer rang as it was very loud. I picked the receiver up and the punter said, 'I'm here! I rang earlier!' I buzzed him in and rushed into the sitting room, where Alice was putting her shoes on.

'He's here, Alice, our first punter!' I quickly reminded her of the basic rates and said if he wanted anything special to come and ask me.

'But I don't do A-levels, or O without, Truly.'

I didn't have time to answer because the punter was knocking on the door. I led him through to the bedroom, where he told me he just wanted a good straight fuck.

While Alice was busy with the punter, Paul came back. I was dying to know how he had got on, so with the sitting room door slightly ajar in case Alice had any trouble I listened to his little adventure. Despite police being everywhere he had managed to card up thirty boxes, but it was the community cops that gave him the most concern. He wondered why most of the telephone boxes had piles of ripped up cards on the floor. At first he thought it was either irate local residents or card men throwing old ones away to put up new ones. Then in Charlotte Street he saw some community cops pulling all the cards off and ripping them up. As they were only stuck on with little blobs of Blu-Tack they were quick to remove.

Paul walked a safe distance behind and followed them as they continued along Charlotte Street, ripping up the cards in all the telephone boxes. I realised this was going to be a big problem. It meant the telephone boxes needed to be carded up more than once a day, and that was going to put Paul at even more risk. He continued to do his best and put the cards out once a day, and we picked up a few punters. I was very grateful to him. Even though I wasn't making any money yet, it meant Alice went home with cash and she was happy to work the next day.

Paul's job as a card man was very short-lived. After just three days I received a call from an angry man with a strong East London accent.

'Who's putting cards in my boxes?'

'I am, but I'm happy for you to do it.'

He completely changed his tune and said, 'That's okay, darling. I understand you're new to the area and I'll be happy to help you.'

After a little more chat, I arranged to meet him at a coffee shop in Tottenham Court Road.

Chapter 26

I instantly liked Carl. He was a bit rough, but he came across as a genuine bloke. He began by asking me how long I'd been in the game. When I told him, he proceeded to fill me in on all the London news and how things worked. It wasn't good news. Carl said I couldn't have chosen a worse time to move to London. Not only were the police raiding flats and closing them down at an alarming rate due to the clean-up ahead of the 2012 Games, but the recession was also beginning to have an effect and many flats were having to slash their prices. Gone were the days of charging what you liked; even the escort industry was suffering and prices were as low as eighty pounds an hour for an outcall. He told me you can make money fast if you're prepared to take big risks by selling drugs to punters and having several girls at the flat offering cheap sexual services, but it comes at a price and your luck never lasts long in this game. No matter how careful you are it's only a matter of time before the police catch up with you.

Carl sensed my disappointment and went on to say, 'Trust me, Truly, I've been in this business for over twenty years. I've been to prison more than once, and seen plenty of others go down since it became an offence to put cards in telephone boxes.'

'But what should I do? I've spent a small fortune coming here.'

'You can still make a good living.'

While digesting Carl's bad news, he explained how he could get my flat going. He took a small London map out of his pocket and showed me how far the Tottenham Court Road area stretched. There were fifty telephone boxes and Carl charged ten pounds per hundred cards. So in order to keep the telephone boxes topped up three times a day, with two different cards in each box to increase the chance of punters choosing one of mine, he'd need three hundred cards a day.

He suggested I start off with one area and if I wanted to expand to another, such as Oxford Street and beyond, then I just had to give him more cards (and money of course) and he would get one of his blokes that worked for him to do it.

Carl wanted to start putting my cards out the following morning, but when I told him I didn't have enough because I'd been printing them on my PC, he gave me the telephone number of a printer called Steve who all the other flats used. Steve charged one hundred and twenty pounds for five thousand cards. He usually delivered them to your flat two days later.

I wanted to get the ball rolling, so while Carl had a cigarette I rang Steve. As soon as I said Carl had given me his number and was sitting across from me he asked to speak to him. I handed the phone over, and Carl confirmed I needed cards a.s.a.p. and handed the phone back. Steve gave his email address and said if I sent the pictures that evening with the telephone number I wanted to use, he'd print and deliver them tomorrow night for one hundred and fifty pounds cash.

Steve did a brilliant job and the cards looked fantastic. Before using the photos I rang Brooke and got her permission to use a couple of her professional portfolio pictures. She agreed as long as I didn't use any facial shots, so I chose a side shot of her naked on all fours with her long hair covering her face, and a rear shot of her holding a riding whip wearing PVC thigh boots and a black thong.

After paying Steve and seeing him out of the door, Carl popped round as arranged to collect the cards so he could get them in the boxes first thing in the morning.

When he saw them he said, 'These are really good pictures.'

'Do you think so?'

'Just get ready for your phone to ring tomorrow.'

We then sat on the sofa and Carl put a couple of piles of each picture on the coffee table. It was like watching a professional croupier as he swiftly counted out and mixed the cards together into piles, each containing one hundred cards.

'I'm going to take enough cards for a couple of days.'

'Why don't you take more so you don't have to keep coming back?'

'Cos it's not good to have too many in case the police stop me, and you shouldn't keep too many at the flat either.'

'Why?'

'Cos the cops will confiscate the lot if they raid you. Then you'll be out of action for a couple of days while Steve prints more.'

I was sure he was right, but I couldn't carry home over four thousand cards. They were far too heavy, so they'd have to stay at the flat. Carl insisted on walking me to the station because it was getting late. He became concerned when I said I was walking to the station on my own because I'd let Alice go home earlier.

'You have to be careful! Never leave the flat on your own, especially when you're going home late.'

'I'm okay, Carl, I can look after myself.'

'You're not in the sticks now. There are fucking scum around here that mug women in the trade cos they know you carry cash, and the chances are you won't report them to the police. Some of them even send their girlfriends to work at the flat for a bit to find out what goes on and how much they're taking. Then they pose as a punter and rob the gaff.'

As we walked along Tottenham Court Road, Carl told me a very disturbing story about one of the flats he used to card up for. Three Somali men, carrying knives, forced their way in, and when the maid stupidly refused to tell them where the money was kept, two of the men went into the bedrooms where both girls were busy with punters. They then robbed the punters and told them to get dressed and leave, after which they raped the girls. If that wasn't bad enough, on their way out one of the men cut off the tip of the maid's nose.

By the time I reached home it was nearly midnight and the house was in darkness. After a cup of tea and settling the dogs down, I crept into bed. My partner didn't even stir when I slid in next to him. Since working with my uncle and having to get up at five thirty he was very tired. Most nights he was in bed by ten o'clock and snoring within minutes. It took quite some time before I was overcome by sleep as my mind was so active. I wondered what tomorrow would bring now that Carl was working for me.

Chapter 27

The day got off to a bad start. I arrived at the flat to discover the bath full of black, greasy, stinky water. I had no idea where it was coming from, but guessed there was some kind of blockage in one of the flats. I rang Raymond, and he promised to get the maintenance man out to me a.s.a.p. I only hoped that he would arrive and sort the problem out before the punters started ringing.

Alice was the first to arrive. 'What's that horrible smell, Truly?'

'Come and see.'

As soon as I opened the bathroom door, Alice shrieked, 'That's disgusting! What is it?'

'Never mind the smell, run and get a saucepan from the kitchen. It's rising, and I need to empty some down the loo before it overflows.' I had managed to empty half of it when the sex phone rang. 'We can't have any punters here until this is sorted.'

'Answer it, Truly. We can just pull the shower curtain across to hide it.'

While I spoke to the punter, Alice lit a couple of scented candles, and placed one in the bathroom and the other in the hallway.

She laughed when I said, 'If anyone complains, we'll just have to pretend that the previous punter had a stinky shit before he left.'

'What if a punter wants a shower?'

'Oh well, just say showers cost extra and hope he's too tight to pay.'

Carl popped in for an update on how things were going. He wasn't at all bothered by the horrible stench and, laughing, said, 'When you've been to as many knocking-shops as I have you get used to the smells.' He was pleased that I had four punters so soon. 'You'll need to get another girl. Punters like choice, even if one's ugly.'

'Yes, I know, Carl, but you know what girls are like. If there's not enough work, they don't come back.'

'Fuck them, Truly. So what if they don't come back? There's plenty more to replace them.'

'Do you think so?'

'Yeah, course. Just use them like they use you. When things pick up you'll be able to hold on to the good girls, but till then don't worry if you can't make them happy. It's the way of the game.'

Next morning, the maintenance man sorted the blockage before we opened up. A waste pipe was completely blocked with fat from the flat next door.

I took Carl's advice, and over the next few weeks went through several girls. Except for one, none of them came back. Chanelle was a pretty twenty-six year old of West Indian origin. She'd rung and asked to do a working interview. I explained we had only recently opened and were having both good and bad days. As long as she understood that I couldn't guarantee what the day would bring, I could offer her Friday.

As with all the girls, we tried to make her feel welcome. We offered food and drinks, and tried to engage in conversation with her, but she refused our hospitality and spent most of the time on her mobile in the bathroom.

Alice didn't like her and said, 'There's something secretive going on. Why doesn't she want us to hear her telephone conversations?'

'I don't know. Maybe she's shy.'

I didn't want a bad atmosphere, so I told Alice to carry on being nice to Chanelle, despite her mistrust. Lunchtime brought the usual punters wanting quick sex. It never ceased to amaze me how men's minds worked; even when at work, they couldn't resist the temptation to have sex. In my opinion it wasn't their fault. They were born with a dick and had the primitive urge to stick it in anything. Plenty of men that came to see us loved their partners and had perfectly good sex lives with them, but they liked the feel of something new. Even though they were being unfaithful, I believed having sex with a working girl was far less damaging to a relationship than having an affair because of the lack of emotional involvement.

Chanelle didn't seem bothered that she wasn't chosen by any of the lunchtime punters. She just sat quietly while Alice had one after another. Towards the evening we noticed a change in her behaviour, and she became very chatty and friendly. At five o'clock she went in the bedroom and came out five minutes later wearing a black and red basque, stockings and high heels.

When I asked why she had changed, she said, 'I needed to.'

At that moment the phone rang and the punter asked if I had any black girls working. I described Chanelle and gave him the address.

I didn't think there was anything strange about the call because punters often wanted to know if I had girls of different origins. I merely put it down to coincidence. Chanelle happened to be there at the right time. It was only after I took another two calls from punters asking the same question, and both of them making an appointment, that I became suspicious. What I couldn't understand was why she didn't tell me that she'd given some regular punters of hers my number. It became quite clear what she was up to after all three punters spent more time in the bedroom than the half hour they'd paid for. The first time I politely and quietly reminded her of the time at the closed bedroom door.

When the punter finally left, I asked what she was doing and she said, 'I couldn't see the bedside clock. It was facing the wall.'

The second time, Carl happened to turn up for a chat and to collect some more cards. When I told him what was going on, he said, 'She's using your gaff for her own punters, and charging them a lot more for extras.'

I banged on the door and insisted the punter get dressed and leave immediately. I knew if he got difficult Carl was there to help me. He had offered his help before. He said if I ever needed him to throw a punter out he or one of his men were never more than a few minutes away. He was now seconds away, having a tea in the kitchen.

Not surprisingly I had to open the bedroom door and ask her third punter to leave. I decided enough was enough. I paid Chanelle, even though I didn't think she deserved it. After all, she had earned far more than I had.

When she asked if she could work next week, I replied, 'I don't think so.'

The following Friday I left Alice at the flat while I popped to the bank.

I was standing in the queue when Alice rang and said, 'Truly, you're not going to believe it. Chanelle has just buzzed on the door.'

'What's she doing? I didn't say she could work again.'

'I know, I told her.'

'What did she say?'

'She wasn't happy. She started swearing.'

'Okay, I'll be back in a few minutes. Don't let her in if she rings again.'

As I made my way back to the flat the phone rang.

'You fucking bitch, I've spent money coming here today.'

'Do you honestly think I would let you work again after your behaviour?'

'What are you on about? I brought some business your way.'

'I'm sorry, but I need girls I can trust.'

She continued to shout and even threatened to tell the police about the flat. I decided I'd heard enough and disconnected her.

For the next few days Alice and I continued to work the flat. One of the cards was generating calls from punters wanting domination and, even though the flat wasn't suitable, we managed to offer mild domination, such as role play, and tie and tease.

Alice loved assisting me, and when I told her I was thinking of getting a bigger flat so we could have a dungeon, she said, 'I'd love to be a dominatrix. Then I wouldn't have to do sex.'

I knew what she meant, as I felt the same. Even though I hadn't personally offered sexual services for some time, I was getting tired of trying to find the girls to do it and the money wasn't as good as domination.

I started thinking. If I opened a flat for domination I could ask Brooke to come back. Alice also had the potential to become a convincing mistress. She had the body of a goddess and a very sexy accent that most punters thought was Russian, even though she was actually Romanian.

It was nearly time to go home when I took a call from a man wanting humiliation and domination. He was reluctant to talk on the phone, so I gave him the prices and address, and told him to come and see us. He soon arrived, and it was the first time I'd ever heard a fantasy like his. He wanted verbal humiliation, spitting and suffocation. That in itself wasn't unusual, it was what he wanted me to call him. After taking his money and telling him to get undressed, I went into the sitting room and explained to Alice what he wanted. She thought it was hilarious and couldn't stop laughing.

I told her, 'I know it's a bit odd, but we have to be serious. Now come on, let's get this over with so we can go home.'

We went into the bedroom and I said to him, 'Pinocchio, you've been telling lies, haven't you?'

'Yes, mistress.'

I spat in his face, grabbed an ear and dragged him over to the bed.

'Lie on the bed face up, you liar!'

'Please, mistress. I'm sorry, mistress.'

'Alice, handcuff his hands and legs to the bed.'

As she bent over to cuff him, she spat in his mouth and called him an ugly piece of shit. Once he was restrained, I took a pillow and held it over his face. Alice looked alarmed because she'd never seen me do that before. I held it firmly for about thirty seconds and then spat in his face again. I repeated the procedure several times, along with verbal abuse from Alice. I can't say I was enjoying what I was doing, but he clearly did because his dick was rock hard and dribbling.

'Alice, remove your knickers!' I screwed them up and shoved them in his mouth. 'Alice, remove one of the handcuffs!' I placed the pillow back over his face and sat on it.

He began to wank like crazy while Alice and I called him a liar. Thankfully, he came before I suffocated him. When Alice released the cuffs, he quickly got dressed, muttered thank you and left.

'He was so weird, Truly. What do you think happened in his life to make him want that done to him?'

'I don't know, and I really don't want to know. Let's go home.' My reaction was exactly the same as Alice when I first started. I was always trying to analyse why someone wanted to be treated so horribly and how it aroused them, but now I didn't really care. I had become desensitised to most of their perversions. Alice had studied psychology in Romania so maybe she'd always be interested in their sick minds.

Chapter 28

The long days were beginning to take their toll and I was feeling exhausted, but until I could find a trustworthy receptionist I had to put in the hours. One morning I didn't need to be in until quite late to interview a young lady named Chloe who'd phoned a couple of days before. I'd given Alice the morning off so she could be with her husband. He was complaining that he was bored in England and was thinking of going back to Romania. From what she told me I figured he was a lazy young man who encouraged her to sell herself so he could spend the money in the betting shop. Alice mentioned that he'd initially come to England on his own. For a couple of weeks he worked as a male escort but gave it up because he hated fucking old women. Shortly after Alice came over to be with him he persuaded her to work in a flat. I never said a word because she was in love with him and I didn't want to upset her, but in my opinion he was a complete loser.

That morning I didn't hear the alarm and woke up just in time to pack George off to school before he missed the taxi that picked him up from the house. It was fortunate that after moving to a different town, the school he attended still sent a taxi to pick him up and drop him home at the end of the day. Henry was more independent because he'd recently passed his driving test (after the fourth attempt) and had saved enough money from his first job to buy a second-hand car.

I was very proud of how responsible the boys were and everything in the house was running smoothly. Henry had taken on the role of cooking dinner for the three of them along with feeding the dogs, while George washed the dishes and vacuumed the house. Nevertheless, I couldn't help feeling guilty about the number of hours I had to work, but until I made enough profit to hire a receptionist I had no option.

I had just enough time to give the flat a quick clean before Chloe arrived. I'd forgotten to empty the condom bin the night before, so I double-bagged the contents and put it in the spare kitchen cupboard until later. I couldn't put the bag in the flat's dustbin because the council checked them if they had any suspicions that the flat was being used as a brothel, so every night on my walk to the station I deposited the bag in one of the many bins along the road.

Chloe's interview coincided with the arrival of a punter, but instead of losing business I threw her in at the deep end. He wanted humiliation and spanking, playing an office role-play scenario where I was the female boss and he a new employee. Despite the fact that Chloe had just arrived and barely had a chance to ask any questions about the job, she didn't hesitate when I asked her to assist me.

After taking the punter into the bedroom and relieving him of two hundred quid, I went back to the sitting room where Chloe was waiting and briefed her on what she needed to do. She went into the bedroom and I listened at the door as Chloe accused him of sexually harassing her.

Thankfully he got into the role straight away and said, 'Please don't tell the boss. I'll do anything to keep my job.'

Chloe was clearly a born little actress and continued to deliver her lines without faltering. After listening for about five minutes, when she demanded he lick the soles of her shoes clean, I banged on the door.

Chloe shouted, 'Come in.'

'What's going on in here, Chloe?'

'This man has been groping my bottom, boss.'

'Has he indeed? Well, I think it's time to teach him a lesson.'

'What shall we do to him?'

'Give him a taste of his own medicine, of course. Now pull down his trousers and pants.'

Chloe looked at me and was trying hard not to laugh by biting her cheeks.

'Bend over the bed, you dirty little pervert.'

'I'm sorry, boss, I won't do it again.'

'Shut up! Chloe, would you like to do the honours?'

'Oh, I'd love to.'

I handed her a large leather paddle and told her to give him a dozen whacks. After a couple of strokes he started wanking and Chloe, noticing what he was doing, continued to spank him harder and harder until he came.

'Thank you, Chloe. You may leave the room.'

The punter thanked me, and said he'd never had two mistresses in the room at the same time and had really enjoyed himself. After showing him out the door I went into the sitting room and found Chloe giggling.

'Well, Chloe, what do you think?'

'I've never had an interview like it.'

'So, does that mean you'd like the job?'

'Not 'arf. I can't wait. This place is going to be a laugh.'

'How many days would you like to work?'

'As many as I can, please.'

After discussing the rates and asking her a few questions about her experience, and her dos and don'ts, I told her I was having great difficulty finding regular girls so I could offer her as many days as she wanted for the time being.

She asked, 'Will I be the only girl here?'

'No. You'll be working with Alice. She should be here soon, if you want to hang around.'

'If it's okay with you I'll meet her tomorrow cos I really have to go now.'

'No problem. Can you be here tomorrow at eleven?'

'Yeah sure, I can't wait.'

Along with Chloe came a kettle and kitchen chaos. She'd noticed at her interview that I was using a saucepan to boil water, so as she passed Robert Dyas on Tottenham Court Road she decided to buy me a kettle. When I offered to give her the money she refused to take it and said the kettle was a gift. I was quite touched by this, as most of the girls I'd dealt with were very mean-spirited.

The kitchen had only been used to make tea and warm up ready-made meals, but with Chloe working at the flat we had constant home-cooked meals. She loved her food, and when she wasn't seeing a punter she spent the rest of her time cooking for us. Besides meals at the flat, eating out at the many cafés and restaurants in the area became a way of rewarding ourselves for working hard, or if one of us had dealt with a horrible punter.

I often wondered, as we sat around a café table laughing about the perverts and punters we'd seen, if any of the locals knew what we did for a living. We certainly didn't come across as sad, desperate women having to sell ourselves like those portrayed in the media. We were actually enjoying ourselves and getting paid extremely well for it. In fact, we often raised our glasses in a toast saying, 'Cheers to punters.'

Over the following weeks I noticed a steady increase in business. The majority of it was for domination, which was surprising because the flat was totally unsuitable. You could hardly swing a cat in there let alone a cat-o'-nine-tails. I would have expected most domination punters to turn around and walk out the door when they saw how unequipped we were, but apart from one or two, the majority of them stayed. The frustrating thing was that if I'd had a bigger flat we could've advertised that we had a dungeon and charged more for the session.

The girls had proved capable and were happy to have a go at most things, knowing I was around to teach them. Chloe had already given a punter a strap-on service and another one a prostate examination. Alice seemed to relish giving pain: electrics and ball busting were her favourites. Whenever a punter asked to have his balls kicked she simply treated the session like she was playing football.

The three of us had the opportunity of having some fun with a punter one morning. The only questions he asked on the phone were the combined weight of the girls and the address.

When I told the girls Chloe laughed and said, 'Maybe he has a fat girl fetish.'

But Alice pointed out, 'No, he would have asked our individual weight.'

Chloe asked, 'What do you reckon, Truly?'

'Fuck knows. Maybe he wants to be squashed.'

I wasn't far off with my guess. The punter turned up and, after literally weighing us all up, he paid for us to ride him around the flat.

The girls went into a fit of giggles when he said in a very posh voice, 'Please, ladies, I want to remain fully clothed.'

For the next half hour I watched as the poor pathetic sod struggled to carry the girls around the flat on all fours. I prayed he wouldn't have a heart attack on the spot; punters leaving the flat in body bags wouldn't be good for business. We laughed like a pack of hyenas when, after unzipping his trousers and taking his cock out without his permission, he politely but firmly told me to put it back. I don't know if he came in his pants or if he was making grunting noises from the sheer weight when I joined the girls riding him, but shortly after he wanted us to get off him.

After he left we all collapsed on the sofa in fits of laughter.

'Oh, Truly, did you see his face when you got his dick out?' asked Alice.

'Yeah, he wasn't happy about it.'

'Do you think he came?' asked Chloe.

'I'm not sure, but it's the easiest money we've earned so far. Changing the subject, I need to talk to you both about Judy.'

'Who's Judy?' asked Chloe.

'She's a girl that used to work for me in Kent. She phoned this morning as I was on my way here and asked if she could work at the flat.'

Chloe said, 'I don't mind having a day off if it helps.'

'Are you sure?'

'I'm earning enough money. Besides, it would be nice to have a day off in the week to catch up on things,' she said. 'And I don't mind having alternate weeks off.'

'Okay great, we can sort out a rota.'

Judy was so excited when I phoned and told her she could have one day a week.

'I won't let you down, I promise.'

'I hope not, Judy. I'll meet you at eleven o'clock on Wednesday outside Warren Street Station, try not to be late.'

Chapter 29

Carl called in after lunch for a cup of tea and to collect some more cards. I noticed he wasn't his usual joking self, and after making him a cup of tea he told me what was going on. One of his men had been arrested for putting up cards in Oxford Street. Pedro was the only one willing to risk the street. Everyone else, including Carl, refused to do it because of the number of CCTV cameras there.

I was sorry to hear about Pedro, but he was a grown man and knew the risks involved. I didn't say anything to Carl, but I was seriously concerned about how it was going to affect work. For the past couple of weeks I'd been giving him an extra two hundred cards a day to do the Oxford Street area and in that time business had picked up. When he left I told the girls about Pedro being arrested and that he was the only one willing to risk Oxford Street.

Alice said, 'Why don't you phone that guy who left a text?'

'What guy?'

'Don't you remember? He's a card man.'

I took the phone and looked through the messages. It was still there, which was surprising because I usually deleted most of them right away—Carl had told me the police often seized mobile phones when they raided to check messages for incriminating evidence.

When I rang the number, a foreign man answered and must have recognised my number because he immediately said, 'Do you want cards putting out?'

'Yes, I do.'

'Shall I call round now? My name is Alpha. I know your address.'

There seemed no point in meeting him at a café if he already knew where my flat was. He must have rung and pretended to be a punter just to find out. Alpha turned up an hour later and fortunately we didn't have any punters, so we were able to chat without fear of being overheard.

After asking him what experience he had of carding up I agreed to give him a two-week trial, partly because I wasn't convinced he was as experienced as he made out, and also I knew Carl was trying to find a replacement for Pedro. While Alice and Chloe counted and mixed together two hundred cards, Alpha sat on the sofa next to me and bragged about the amount of work he had in the Tottenham Court Road area. I was sure he was talking bullshit, because I knew Carl wouldn't tolerate anyone working on his patch. When he left we all agreed he was a liar and that we shouldn't trust him with the job. We decided from the next day to ask all the punters where they were calling from.

Later in the day we had a punter wanting a strap-on service. After showing him both girls he paid the fee and then took a coin out of his pocket.

'Heads for Alice, tails for Chloe.'

It landed on the bed tails up.

'Chloe will be in to see you in a minute, okay?'

Chloe's face dropped when I told her the punter had chosen her to fuck him.

'Why do I get all the dirty jobs?'

'Never mind, Chloe, just think of the money,' Alice commented.

Poor Chloe! I couldn't help feeling sorry for her. She came out of the bedroom twenty minutes later and asked if I could show him out after he'd used the bathroom. Judging by the look on her face the session had been messy. As soon as I'd showed the punter out, she shouted, 'Don't come in here, girls, the room stinks.'

We ignored her, and walking in I said, 'Pooh! Open the window please, Alice.'

'I'm sorry about the mess, Truly, I couldn't help it. He was full of poo.'

'Don't worry about it. It's not your fault.'

We quickly changed the bedding and washed the floor. Fortunately it was laminate and easy to clean up with a bucket of disinfectant. After a spray round the room with air freshener, the smell had disappeared.

I asked Chloe, 'What did you do with the strap-on?'

'I put it to soak in the bathroom, with a drop of disinfectant.'

'Why? Did you forget to put a condom on it?'

'No. But the shit went higher than the condom.'

'Now you know why I told you to wear a couple of pairs of knickers.'

'I'm glad you did, cos if I hadn't it would have gone all over me.'

The rest of the day passed fairly uneventfully, with the usual flow of punters wanting straight sex. I was getting tired of sitting in the hallway on the fisherman's chair. Maybe it was time to move now that we were seeing an increase in punters. I searched for Raymond's number on my personal mobile phone. I told him I needed to move to a larger flat and asked if he had any in the area.

'I hate to say it, but I haven't got anything suitable right now.'

'Are you sure, Raymond?'

'Well, I might have one, but it's considerably more than what you're paying.'

'How much is it?'

'It's eight hundred a week, plus bills.'

'That seems a bit expensive. How big is it?'

'Two bedrooms.'

'I'll have a think about it.'

'Okay, just give us a ring if you want to look at it.'

Later that night, on our way home, we walked along Fitzroy Street towards Goodge Street Station so I could have a look in a few estate agents' windows. I noticed a flat in my block for three hundred a week so I knew I was paying a premium, even with the bills included. I was paying about a hundred and fifty pounds too much and wondered who was pocketing the difference: Raymond, Marvin or the landlord.

It didn't surprise me that I was being ripped off. Ever since being in the business I had come across men wanting a slice of the pie, from website designers and advertisers to punters dangling carrots in return for sexual favours. They assumed that because I ran a knocking-shop I was easy and had money to burn. Far from it; since being involved in the sex industry I'd lost interest in sex, and as for money I still hadn't recouped all I'd spent.

The train journey home was slower than usual, with the train stopping at every station. I had to resist the urge to sleep; after what Carl had told me about muggings I never let my guard down. The train finally pulled into my hometown and I walked the short distance to my car. I felt sad when I pulled up on the driveway. The house was yet again in darkness, which meant another night of not seeing the boys. I wondered if anyone was going to benefit from what I was doing. Only time would tell. I sent a text to Judy reminding her of our meeting the next morning, switched off the bedside lamp and quickly drifted off to sleep.

While I stood outside the station waiting for Judy, Carl came along.

'What're you doing, Truly?'

'I'm waiting for one of my girls.'

'Don't forget to keep an eye on that Alpha, cos I've heard he's a waste of space.'

'Who told you that?'

'A couple of flats gave him a go and then found out he was missing a lot of the boxes.'

'I'll probably have a walk around Oxford Street in a few days to make sure he's putting them everywhere.'

'Okay, I'd better go now. I'll call in later for some more cards.'

A couple of minutes later Judy arrived looking frazzled.

'Hi, Truly, sorry I'm late, the train was delayed.'

'Not to worry. The phone hasn't started ringing yet.'

'I'm so excited about working in London. How busy is the flat?'

'It's not bad considering its small. You'll see in a minute, it's just around the corner. Come on, let's hurry, it's about to rain.'

We ran the last couple of hundred yards to avoid getting drenched. Judy was so eager to get inside she tried to open the glass entrance doors.

'They won't open till I enter the code.' While I punched in the numbers, Judy squashed her nose up against the glass like a small inquisitive child.

'Oh, Truly, it's so posh with all the mirrors and black marble. I bet you get a lot of rich punters here.'

'Well, Judy, you know what it's like in this game. Just because they're rich, it doesn't mean they're not tight. But we have had a few generous ones, including an eminent MP and a famous footballer.'

Alice nearly jumped out of her skin when I opened the sitting room door. I'd given her a spare key about a week before so she could let herself in if she arrived before me.

'Wow, Truly, you really made me jump.'

'I'm sorry, Alice, I should have rung the bell.'

'I didn't hear you come in cos of the TV.'

'Oh, by the way, this is Judy.'

'Hi, Judy, I'm Alice.'

'Hello, Alice, Truly has told me about you.'

'Okay, girls, let's have a cup of tea before the phone kicks off.'

'Shall I make it, Truly?'

'Yes please, Alice. While you're doing that I'll show Judy the flat.'

Judy loved the black and red colour scheme in the bedroom. 'It's so classy, Truly. Even the towels are black and red, and I just love the red scented candles. It all looks so sexy.'

'Thanks, Judy. Alice helped me with the finishing touches, and the great thing is the punters love it. Come on now, the tea must be ready.'

It was lovely sitting with the girls on the reclining sofa, drinking tea and munching chocolate biscuits while filling Judy in on all the London news. Not long after finishing our tea, the phone rang.

'Here we go, girls.'

'Come on, Judy, let's get ready.'

The girls trotted off into the bedroom while I gave the details. By the time they'd come back out about ten minutes later, I'd answered another three calls.

'Fingers crossed, girls. I think we're going to have a rush on.'

Alice said, 'Great, let's hope they all turn up.'

Unfortunately for Judy, of the four punters that rang only two turned up and they both chose Alice. Judy started to look for reasons why.

'Do you think I'm dressed okay, Truly?'

'Yes, why are you asking?'

'Well, I don't think I look sexy enough.'

'Do you want my honest opinion?'

'Yeah . . . I think so.'

'You've got too skinny. Are you eating?'

'I do try, but I don't have much of an appetite.'

'It's all the drugs you do.'

I was convinced Judy also suffered from an eating disorder. Brooke told me she had heard her vomiting soon after eating on a couple of occasions at my hometown flat.

'I don't want to upset you, Judy, but if you want to attract real men instead of perverts only interested in childlike bodies you have to feed yourself up. And the best way to do that is to lay off the drugs and maybe get some counselling for your eating disorder.'

'But I don't have an eating disorder, Truly.'

'Are you sure?'

She didn't answer, but by the look on her face I must have touched a nerve.

'When Alice is finished with her punter we'll have a look in the wardrobe. I think one of the girls left a silk negligee behind when we did the photo shoot. If you wear that with a pair of high heels you will look sexier.'

'But I didn't bring any high heels.'

'You can borrow a pair of mine. If they're a bit big we can stuff some loo paper in the toes.'

After showing the punter out, we rummaged through the wardrobe. I was right; there was a lovely little black and pink La Senza negligee in one of the drawers.

Judy said, 'Look, Truly, the price tag is still on it.'

'How much was it?'

'Thirty-five pounds.'

'Try it on with these shoes.'

The outfit did the trick and the next punter chose Judy, much to my relief because I didn't want to see her miserable face any more. I'd put up with enough of that in the previous flat whenever a punter didn't choose her. Hopefully my little chat with her had sunk in.

While Judy was busy, Alice and I chatted about moving.

'Truly, why don't we come here early tomorrow so we can go to the agents down the road?'

'Yes, we could, but we can't very well tell them we want it for a knocking-shop.'

'Of course not. Anyway, they don't need to know.'

'The problem is if the landlord finds out he'll probably chuck us out.'

'I'm sure we could get away with it for six months. After all, we've been here nearly three months and no one's called the police.'

'I suppose there's no harm in looking.'

By the end of the day Alice had seen another three punters and Judy got a punter wanting her to dress as a schoolgirl. She even agreed to be spanked as long as he didn't leave any marks. I turned the television down so I could hear if things were getting out of control. After listening at the door for a few minutes it became apparent the punter was a pretty harmless guy.

'You've been a naughty little girl, so I'm going to pull your knickers down and smack your bottom.' He then told her to lie across his lap and he proceeded to spank her.

Judy responded by saying, 'I'm sorry, sir. Please stop.'

I went back in the sitting room and found Alice sleeping on the sofa.

'Wakey-wakey, Alice.'

'Sorry, Truly, I'm so tired.'

'Why don't you get ready to go home?'

'Can I?'

'Yeah, why not? I could do with an early night myself.'

'What's going on in there?'

'She should be finished soon, the punter's just spanking her bottom.'

I was counting out the money when Judy poked her head round the sitting room door.

'Can you show the gentleman out, please?'

'I'll do it, Truly.'

'Thanks, Alice.'

While we were waiting for Judy to get changed in the bathroom we cleaned the bedroom ready for the next morning.

'What the hell is she doing in there?'

'Go hurry her up, Alice, please.'

'Come on, Judy, hurry up. Truly's going to miss her train.'

'Okay, I'm coming.'

Chapter 30

My train home was so crowded I had to walk through several carriages before managing to find a seat near a group of middle-aged women who were making rather a lot of noise. They looked pretty drunk, and judging by all the laughter they were having a really good time. I felt quite jealous. I couldn't remember the last time I went out with friends. Admittedly the flat wasn't short of laughs, but running a brothel wasn't all it was cracked up to be. Many boring hours were spent sitting around waiting for customers, and the long hours meant a social life was out of the question. The only thing I did when I got home was flop into bed. If I was a lifestyle madam and was happy to socialise with punters outside the workplace, things might be different, but I never mixed business with pleasure.

I'd had more than my fair share of punters wanting to take me out for dinner or on holiday, and a few wanting a serious relationship, but the idea of dating a man I'd met through work didn't appeal to me no matter what he had to offer. I'd find it very hard to trust the man and I'm pretty sure he'd feel the same.

Alice had put a regular punter straight only a few weeks before. After being in the room with her for a few minutes he told her he really wanted to take me out to dinner.

'But Truly doesn't go out with clients.'

'Is that so?'

'Yes, it's true.'

'I bet she would if she knew I had money.'

'Would you like me to ask her?'

'Do it when I've gone. I bet when I come back she'll say yes.'

'What makes you say that?'

'All girls can be bought.'

When Alice told me what he'd said I laughed and said, 'What an arrogant chauvinistic old pig. I wouldn't have him if his arse hung with diamonds.'

When he next paid a visit I told him that in my experience talk comes cheap. Unless he could afford to put his money where his mouth was and be my money-piggy, and lavish me with money and expensive gifts, then he may as well forget it. He must have got the message loud and clear, because the subject was never mentioned again.

As arranged the previous day, Alice was sitting outside the café next door but one to the estate agents. She could have been mistaken for a famous actress as she sat at the table. Wearing a pair of large sunglasses she was taking deep drags on her cigarette and then slowly exhaling clouds of smoke. Her long shapely legs were crossed and casually resting on the chair opposite, and for a brief moment I envied her youth and beauty as she basked in the morning sun.

'Morning, Alice, I'm going to get a coffee before we go to the agents. Do you want another?'

'Yes, thanks, Truly, I'll have a cappuccino.'

We went and had a quick look in the agent's window while waiting for the coffee. Alice pointed out a two-bedroom Georgian flat spread over two floors in the Fitzrovia area for five hundred pounds a week.

'It looks nice, Truly.'

'Yes, it does. I'm sure we walk past that building when we go to the Italian restaurant.'

'You're right. I think it's on Warren Street.'

'Come on, the coffee's arrived.'

We sipped the coffee and planned what we were going to say to the agent. I felt it a good idea to say I worked from home as a trichologist specialising in male baldness, so I had several clients visiting during the day and a few in the evenings. Hopefully by confessing to running this kind of business the agency and landlord were less likely to become suspicious if any of the neighbours reported men coming and going.

After filling out the registration form the agent looked on the computer and found three possible properties within walking distance. Because he held the keys, and all were vacant and available for immediate occupancy, I asked if we could view them after lunch.

'I can do three o'clock.'

'That's fine.'

'If you'd care to meet me outside this one on Rathbone Street we can view it and go on to the others.'

'That's great. See you at three.'

'Oh and you'd better take these brochures; they've got the addresses and a little map.'

As soon as we got outside the estate agents I turned the volume up on the phones. 'Shit! Six missed calls. Come on, we'd better hurry. We're missing business.'

As we approached the flat I could see Chloe sitting on the steps. *Poor girl, I forgot to let her know I'd be late.*

'I'm sorry, Chloe, I should have called you. We've been to the estate agents.'

'That's okay, it's nice in the sun. Anyway, what did you find?'

'Three possible flats I'll be looking at this afternoon.'

'That's really good, hopefully one will be suitable.'

'Yeah, with a bit of luck. Anyway, let's get in, the phone's been ringing.'

It turned out to be a disappointing few hours with not one punter. In that time Carl called round for some cards and a cuppa. From what he said we were not the only ones having a quiet time. Another madam had told him she'd never known it so quiet in all her twenty years of being in the area.

'Why do you think it's gone so quiet, Carl?'

'There are many flats offering cheap sex. A new one has just opened round the corner run by an Albanian bloke with ten girls in it. Mind you, he won't last long when the police get to hear about him.'

'Maybe they won't bother. They haven't with us.'

'Oh, don't speak too soon, Truly. It's only a matter of time.'

'What do you think will happen if they do?'

'You never know with them. They may try to close you straight away, or they might just keep an eye on ya. Anyway, I'll catch ya later, girls.'

'Okay, Carl, take care.'

'By the way, don't forget to check up on Alpha.'

I began to wonder if it was worth looking for another flat. Given the circumstances it was probably best to get out of London. But how could I give up when I'd come this far? No, it was out of the question. I had to give it another six months at the very least.

Chloe offered to stay and answer the phones while we looked at the flats. 'Are you sure you don't want to come with us?'

'No, I'm okay. I'm going to get dinner ready.'

'Okay, we'll try not to be long. If the phone rings, tell them we're busy for the next hour.'

Two of the properties were not suitable as the rooms were far too small for our needs. But the Warren Street flat was nearly perfect. It was spread over the second and third floors of a late Georgian terraced building, and the ground floor had been converted to an office some time ago and had its own entrance. The only problem I could see was sharing the street door and flight of stairs with the first-floor flat.

The flat was generously proportioned with a nice modern bathroom, large sitting room with two sash-windows facing Warren Street and a fabulous kitchen with black granite work surfaces and integrated fridge-freezer, dishwasher, washing machine and a huge cooker. I knew Chloe would be in heaven if she was here.

The upstairs floor had two rooms: one exactly the same size as the sitting room below it and a slightly smaller one overlooking the rear of the property, though it was still large enough for a six-foot wide bed and furniture. I couldn't believe it when the agent opened a door on the landing and showed us a small flight of stairs.

'You even have your own private roof terrace.'

'Can we go up and have a look?'

'I'm sorry, I don't have keys for the hatch yet.'

After having another look around the flat I told the agent I'd get back to him. Alice couldn't contain her excitement as we walked back to work.

'Oh, Truly, it's gorgeous, you just have to take it.'

'Yes, it's lovely, but I'm worried about sharing the stairs with the flat below. I'm going to have to find out who lives there.'

'I'm sure we'll be fine. After all, we don't do twenty-four hours.'

'I know, but I still need to be careful.'

I looked at several other flats over the following couple of days but none were as good as Warren Street for the money. I decided to take it. Because credit checks and employment references were out of the question, I had to agree to pay three months rent up front, along with a six-week deposit. Fortunately, the landlord didn't mind waiting for four weeks when I explained I had to give a month's notice on my other flat and didn't want the tenancy to start until then.

During that month quite a lot happened. Carl was right about Alpha. He turned out to be a complete waste of space. He was missing most of the boxes, so I had to let him go. The police, on the other hand, were doing their job a little too efficiently for my liking. Carl called in for his usual cuppa a little earlier than usual one morning.

'Have you seen the news, Truly?'

'No, why?'

'You need to put it on now!'

Chloe was switching the channel as we spoke.

'What's the problem, Carl?'

'Seven flats got raided last night, and some people were arrested.'

'Where are the flats?'

'I think they're all in the Knightsbridge and Mayfair area.'

'But that's nowhere near here.'

'Yeah I know, but it's still bad news for us cos it means they're purging the place.'

'Why do you say that?'

'Well they don't normally raid seven flats in one night. It's obviously been planned for some time.'

'What should we do?'

'There's nothing you can do, except keep an eye open for anyone watching the place, especially when you open up.'

'Why?'

'Because they like to find out who's got the keys.'

News of the raid came on the screen and two men were shown being led out of a property in handcuffs. The reporter said seven flats had been raided and several arrests made.

'Oh my gosh, I recognise that house. I went for an interview there.'

'When, Chloe?'

'Just before I started here.'

'What happened?'

'I didn't like the idea of working all through the night.'

'What was the madam like?' asked Alice.

'It wasn't a woman, it was some German bloke.'

'I've got to go now, girls. Try not to worry too much, Truly, or you'll just make yourself ill.'

It wasn't all bad news. A week before moving Brooke rang and asked if she could work for me on a Thursday. Since the last time we spoke she'd left Liverpool Street and in her words, 'Went and got a proper job.' She was working in sales, but only four days a week and she needed to earn some extra cash. Like many girls who've worked in the sex industry, including myself, she found it impossible to return to normality for any length of time. There was something about the job that kept luring you back. I don't know if it was the promise of a lot of quick cash or the buzz you got from doing a potentially dangerous job, but whatever the reasons Brooke had they were not my concern. I was pleased to hear from her and knew she would be good for business. With her domination skills she could easily handle the big boys without my help.

Alice and Chloe were learning fast but were not always confident enough to be left in charge of a seasoned dom punter. In my experience that kind of punter had to be treated like a dog; no apprehension or fear to be shown in front of them. Otherwise the fantasy of their mistress controlling and dominating them would quickly evaporate, resulting in a disappointing session for the punter.

Brooke was grinning when I opened the door to her.

'It's a bit weird to see my arse plastered all round London.'

'Well not all of London, I can't afford to pay Carl that much.'

'I can't believe how good it looks.'

'The punters certainly like it. I've even had a few of them asking, "When does the girl with the nice arse work?"'

'Well I'm here now, so you can line them up.'

'It's good to see you, Brooke. Now come and meet Chloe, she's been looking forward to meeting you.'

It didn't take long for Brooke to settle in. It was like she'd never been away, and when Pinocchio turned up again he couldn't have chosen a better day. Brooke delighted in humiliating him. Along with name calling and spitting she even tied rope to his wrists and had him performing like a marionette while she sang along. She'd clearly got it right for him, because when he paid another visit he was only interested in seeing her.

Chapter 31

The moving day finally arrived, and as it was on a Wednesday, Alice and Judy were around to help pack up the few bits and clean the flat. By lunchtime we were ready to go. Raymond turned up as promised to take back the keys and do the checkout inspection. After a quick look round the flat he confirmed that everything was okay and said I'd receive my full deposit back within seven to ten days. We then crammed everything into the lift including the mattress and base, and took it all down to the lobby.

'I suggest we walk round to the flat with the suitcases and boxes, and then come back for the mattress and base.'

'What about the keys for Warren Street?' Alice asked.

'I picked them up on the way in this morning.'

It was very warm that morning and by the time we had climbed the stairs to the flat we were all sweating.

'Come on, girls, let's just shove the stuff in the sitting room and go get the bed.'

'Can I have a look around first?'

'No, come on, Judy, you'll have time when we get back.'

We must have looked amusing struggling along the road with the bed base. It certainly wasn't something normally seen in the Fitzrovia area. On our return to pick up the mattress I decided to hail a taxi because I was out of breath and suffering

from palpitations. I had first developed them a little while after my partner moved in. If I'd taken the cardiologist's advice and avoided the things that brought them on, I probably wouldn't have stayed with my partner and certainly wouldn't be running a knocking-shop.

When we got the mattress outside, Alice said, 'It won't fit, Truly.'

'Yes it will, if we fold it in half.'

The taxi driver laughed and agreed to take us. 'Okay, girls, as it's only around the corner, cos if the Old Bill see I'm overloaded I'll be in trouble.'

I told him, 'You're not the only one that's going to be in the shit if the police find out.'

'What do ya mean?'

I winked and replied, 'Well let's put it this way, we don't use the mattress for sleeping on.'

He smiled and said, 'So, I know where to come when I want some relief.'

'Alice, Judy, come on, fold the mattress up and sit on it. This kind man's going to take us.'

After spending the next hour setting up the flat we were ready for punters. Unfortunately, the dungeon couldn't be set up until the weekend as I needed my partner's help to fetch the heavy items from storage and a van to transport them to the flat. While waiting for the phone to ring we checked out the roof terrace.

I told the girls, 'I think we should have lunch up here.'

'What a good idea,' Alice said. 'It's so lovely and warm.'

Judy said, 'This flat is brilliant. We're so lucky.'

'Judy, can you do me a favour? Pop round to Tesco's and grab something nice for lunch, and a bottle of wine to celebrate. Here's the money. It's my treat.'

The chicken salad washed down with the wine tasted delicious. I'm sure it had more to do with where we were rather than the food itself. There was something quite special about having lunch on one's own private roof terrace.

Over the next couple of weeks the business went from strength to strength and the takings increased by more than fifty per cent. To launch the new premises and services on offer I had several new cards made. The card we had the most fun photographing was the one advertising an adult baby service. I managed to persuade Paul to model as an adult baby with the promise of a good few beers.

The photo shoot started out in a serious way. Paul even brought along a professional photographer friend who specialised in glamour photography because it wasn't his own speciality. After his friend photographed Alice and Chloe it was impossible to keep a straight face when Paul entered the room. He was dressed in a pale blue romper suit I'd bought online from a site for adult babies, and was even sucking on a dummy. During the shoot Chloe posed as Nurse Naughty, and for added excitement Alice joined her dressed as a doctor with a stethoscope. We even did cards for punters with a rubber or PVC fetish. Alice was the perfect model for this with her amazing body. The combination of studio lighting and skin-tight fabrics defining the contours of her perfect breasts and bottom made for some great pictures.

The four-hour photo shoot soon had an effect when the cards were printed and distributed. News travelled fast, and according to Carl we were the talk of the neighbourhood. While the girls in the other flats sat around waiting for punters to turn up, we were thriving. Carl was constantly being asked by other madams what was going on in our flat and why we were so popular. Fortunately for me, he was a closed book when it came to my business. He had come to be my guardian angel and I knew I could trust him. The girls reckoned he was in love with me, but I thought he'd just taken me under his wing.

Punters had also started telling the other flats how good we were. I could only imagine how annoying that must have been, especially if the punter was comparing the difference after having had a poor service. I think the main reason for our success was the atmosphere in the flat. The girls were having fun and that was evident to the punters. It was nothing unusual for the girls to join in on one another's dom sessions just for the hell of it, at no extra cost to the punter.

Chapter 32

A few weeks after moving to Warren Street we had quite an eventful day. It started with Chloe asking, 'What's all that shouting about, Truly?'

'I don't know, but we'd better go and find out.'

The shouting was coming from the dom-room where Alice was supposed to be administering humiliation and corporal punishment to a very well-spoken gentleman.

'When did the punter get here?' Chloe asked.

'About fifteen minutes ago. You were busy in the other room when he arrived. Come on, let's go.'

As we climbed the stairs it became apparent that the raised voices were not part of an act. The punter was shouting angrily at Alice. I stood listening at the door for a few seconds more.

'He's bullying her, Truly! What are you going to do?'

'Watch and learn.'

'But we need Carl.'

'Don't worry, I don't need him for this bully. Now go and grab the large cane from the other room. Quickly, Chloe.'

Armed with the cane and fuelled with adrenaline, I burst into the room. The punter glared at me, grabbed a towel off the whipping bench and wrapped it around himself.

'How dare you come in here, woman?'

Alice stood shaking slightly. She was clearly out of her depth with this bastard and he'd reduced her to tears.

'May I ask what's going on?'

'You're just the bloody maid. Now get out.'

'Alice, what's the problem?'

'He keeps shouting at me and says I'm a useless dominatrix.'

'Oh, does he now?' Even though I could feel my heart pounding in my chest I remained calm on the exterior and automatically went into dominatrix mode. 'Get on your knees!'

'Certainly not.'

Before he knew what was happening, I ripped the towel off him and swiftly brought the cane down as hard as I could over his fat backside. The pain was instant and he hit the floor like a dead man. For a few seconds I watched him as he curled up into the foetal position.

'Now, would you like me to continue with the session, or are you happy with Alice?'

He was clearly in agony because he was unable to talk. I waited for the pain to subside enough for him to be able to answer.

'I'm sorry, mistress, I don't know what came over me. I'm very happy with Mistress Alice.'

'Very well. Alice, you may continue. But if he disrespects you again, call me.'

'Thank you, Truly.'

I glared at the punter, who had only just recovered enough to get up off the floor. I turned round and left the room, where I found Chloe waiting.

'Did you cane him, Truly?'

'Yes, I believe in giving a bully a good beating. It's the only way to deal with them.'

'Are you going to leave Alice on her own?'

'No, we'll sit on the stairs and wait for the session to finish, okay?'

Not long after, the door opened.

'Can you show the gentleman out please, Truly?'

'Yes, of course.' I didn't utter a single word as he followed me down the stairs. I simply opened the door and said, 'Shoo! Off you go,' gesturing with my hand.

By the time I got back upstairs Chloe was in the dom-room where Alice was giving a blow-by-blow account.

'I wish you could have seen what Truly did to him. She was amazing.'

'I was listening at the door and I heard her whack him.'

'Yeah, it was great. She caned him so hard it bled.'

I told her, 'Alice, you must never let things get out of hand like that again.'

'But what could I do?'

'You should have called me when he started to get difficult.'

'Yes, but I thought I could handle him.'

'Well you thought wrong.'

'But he seemed so nice at first.'

'Yeah, so was the Yorkshire Ripper, apparently. Look, girls, never assume that all guys who come for domination are submissive. Some of them are really fucked up in the head. You should know that, Alice, you've got a degree in psychology.'

'She's right, Alice. We have to be wary of them all.'

'Anyway, it's over now, so let's have some lunch,' I told them.

'Good idea, I'm starving.'

Alice laughed when I replied, 'You're always fucking starving, Chloe.'

Lunch was interrupted by the entry buzzer.

'Shit! Why do they always call when we're eating?'

'Don't complain, Chloe, it's money.' I left the kitchen and went to answer it. 'Hello, come on up.'

'I rang earlier. I'm the adult baby.'

'Please don't talk on the doorstep. Just come in, will you?'

'I'm a bit nervous. I've never done this before.'

'That's what they all say, love. Now are you coming in or not?'

'Okay, I'm coming.'

I couldn't understand these men; they say they're nervous but are quite happy to discuss their little peccadilloes on the street where they could quite easily be overheard by passers-by. I'm sure in a lot of cases they didn't have a nervous bone in their body and in fact it was just part of the game.

'Come on, girls, leave your lunch and go upstairs cos we've got to do some babysitting.'

'Oh, I do hope he's potty-trained,' said Chloe.

'Well if he's not we'll charge him extra.'

'Yeah I know, but I don't fancy cleaning him up when I've just been eating.'

'Quickly, girls, he's at the door.'

I was quite surprised when I opened the door to an extremely good-looking man of about forty who was immaculately dressed in a grey suit, blue shirt and tie, with black crocodile shoes.

'It's lovely to meet you, darling. Would you care to follow me?'

'Are you the nanny?'

'No. The ladies are upstairs waiting for you.'

After being introduced to both girls he chose Chloe because he reckoned she looked more mumsy than Alice.

'Okay, would you wait here? Chloe will be in to see you in a few minutes.'

When I went back downstairs Chloe was finishing her lunch. 'You haven't time for that, Chloe. He's chosen you cos he thinks you're more mumsy.'

'Stop laughing, you two, it's not funny.'

Twenty minutes into the session Chloe shouted down the stairs, 'Truly, can you come up here please?'

I could tell by her tone she wasn't in any difficulty. It was just part of the act. I walked in and found Chloe sitting on a blanket on the floor while the punter crawled around in nothing but a pair of plastic pants with a dummy in his mouth. I couldn't help laughing at the transformation. He certainly bore no resemblance to the gentleman I'd met at the door.

'What's the matter, Chloe?'

'He's being naughty, and he says nanny has to spank his botty.'

'Can I have a word in the next room? We don't want to upset the baby.'

Chloe quickly filled me in on what he wanted before going back in the room. When we returned he had his hand down his plastic pants and was wanking.

'Look at the naughty boy, Chloe. He's found his willy.'

'What should we do, nanny?'

'I'm going to put him across my knee and give him a good hard smack.'

He didn't have to be persuaded. As soon as I was seated he ran straight across to me and positioned himself so his hard cock was between my thighs. I was glad he had the plastic pants on, because after only half a dozen smacks with my bare hand he ejaculated. He then spat the dummy out and got up off my knees.

'Thank you so much, ladies. That was most enjoyable.'

'I'm glad you enjoyed yourself. That's what we're here for. Now, if you'd care to get dressed and come downstairs when you're ready. Don't forget, the bathroom's downstairs if you need to use it.'

After he left I asked Alice to make some tea and Chloe said, 'He was quite sweet, wasn't he, Truly?'

'Yeah, he was nice and easy. I wish we had more like him.'

'It's so much easier than doing sex.'

'Let's be honest, we don't do much sex these days.'

'Well I hope we do tomorrow because Judy's in,' noted Alice, 'and you know what she's like if it's quiet.'

Then Chloe said, 'Oh, Truly, I wanted to ask you something.'

'What's that?'

'Would you mind if one of my regular punters, from a flat I used to work in, comes here?'

'No, I don't mind, but how come he has your number?'

'I used to go to his house sometimes.'

'What's he like?' asked Alice.

'He's a real pervert, but he's got plenty of money.'

'What do you have to do to him?' asked Alice again.

'He likes me to jump on him.'

'Is that all?'

'Yeah, pretty much. Sometimes he wanks at the same time.'

'It sounds easy.'

'Well actually it's quite tiring, especially if it's a long session.'

'How much can we get out of him?' I asked her.

'I hope you don't mind, Truly, but I've already told him it's a very posh flat and you charge two fifty an hour.'

'That's good. So when's he coming?'

'I'll let you know when he calls back.'

Later on in the afternoon Alice had a punter wanting to use poppers. Chloe and I were sitting in the kitchen when she came rushing down the stairs.

'What's the matter, Alice?'

'I need the poppers from the fridge.'

'It's all gone. Brooke used it all up last week.'

'Shit! He says he doesn't want the session without the poppers.'

'Don't worry, go and tell him the maid will jump in a taxi to get some.'

A few minutes later Alice came back downstairs with a hundred and fifty pounds for the session plus an extra twenty for the poppers.

'Okay, I'm going right now. Do me a favour, Chloe, look after Alice, and don't let anyone else in unless it's Carl.'

I managed to wave a taxi down as soon as I was out of the door.

'Where to, love?'

'The sex shop in Goodge Street.'

'What?'

'I'm not joking.'

'You're in a bit of a hurry, darling. Don't you have time to walk?' He was obviously enjoying himself trying to embarrass a middle-aged woman for going to a sex shop.

'No, I don't have time, cos I'm fucking busy and vice versa.'

'But it's spitting distance.'

'Look, if you must know I run a knocking-shop and I'm out of poppers. So now you've had the ins and outs of a maggot's arse, perhaps you could shut your mouth and put your foot down.'

'Okay, keep your hair on, luv, we're here now.'

'Wait here, please. I need you to take me back.'

Thankfully, the only time the driver spoke on the return journey was when we pulled up outside the flat and he asked me for the fare.

After running the poppers up to Alice I went into the kitchen and found Carl drinking a cup of tea.

'Alright, Truly? Did you get the poppers?'

'Chloe told you.'

'Yeah, she asked me to wait till you got back.'

'Where is she?'

'Upstairs with a punter, he buzzed a few minutes ago. She said he's a regular.'

'Is it sex or dom?'

'Sex, I think. She said he was a professor.'

'Oh, that's the one that tries to please her in bed.'

Carl laughed when I told him a story about a punter that wanted to please me. I lost my patience after hearing him continually asking what pleased me, and when I told him the only thing that pleases me is counting the money at the end of the day so he may as well get on with pleasing himself, he shut up and got on with the job.

'Thanks for stopping, Carl.'

'No problem, Truly. I'm quite happy to help, you know that.'

'What's going on in the other flats?'

'They're all fucking quiet. It's a good job you do dom.'

'Yeah, we'd have died a long time ago if we didn't.'

'Do you ever leave the pervs on their own?'

'Sometimes, why do you ask?'

'Well, do you ever suspend them, or wrap them in plastic and leave them alone?'

'Not really, why?'

'Since I've been in this game I've seen two deaths. One was when an old man of about eighty tripped over and smacked his head on the corner of the fireplace . . .'

'How did he manage that?'

'The silly old sod tripped up on the rug when he was about to spank the girl's arse.'

'How do you know about it? It might be bullshit.'

'You're joking, Truly. I was there at the time, and the girl was screaming her head off.'

'What happened?'

'We called the police. No choice.'

'Did she get arrested?'

'No. After they spoke to us and forensics turned up, they could tell it was just an accident.'

'Did the flat get closed down?'

'No. The woman moved before the police could do anything. She's got a flat in the Victoria area now.'

'What was the other death?'

'That happened years ago when I was picking up cards from a dominatrix, not far from here. The silly cow forgot about the pervert she'd suspended. By the time she went and looked he was blue.'

'What did you do?'

'I took one look at him and fucked off. Can you blame me?'

'But how come he was blue?'

'It looked like the waist support broke so the neck suspension hung him.'

'Oh my God, what happened to her?'

'I'm not sure. I think she got off with accidental death, but it finished her.'

'I'm not surprised.'

'Anyway, Truly, just make sure you don't leave them on their own, especially if you're doing anything dodgy.'

'Don't worry, Carl. I don't want anyone leaving here in a body bag.'

His stories might have sounded amusing, but a death at the flat was always a possibility. Most of our customers were middle-aged unfit men who probably had high blood pressure and a certain amount of heart disease. With the levels of excitement they reached a heart attack was quite possible. I often wondered what I should do if a tragedy happened, and had even spoken to my solicitor about the possibility of being sued by a grieving relative. I could hardly protect myself by taking out liability insurance to cover a knocking-shop. Yet again, this was another side to the business that left me vulnerable.

Later on I had a little chat with the girls concerning what Carl had told me. Their initial reaction was to laugh. Alice even suggested that if a punter died on the job we could all dress him up before we called the ambulance. That way, she stupidly thought, we could deny having anything to do with him. I knew we couldn't prevent a heart attack, but we could take his advice and never leave a punter alone if he was tied up or having any kind of asphyxiation treatment.

Chapter 33

As if I didn't have enough to worry about, a couple of days after talking to Carl about the deaths, our neighbours downstairs moved out. I didn't think we were the reason for the sudden departure, because the two guys had always been friendly with us and they were hardly ever home. What worried me was who we were going to get instead.

I decided to make the most of the situation while the flat remained empty by extending our opening hours. As always, Carl offered to help. He looked after the girls in the morning while I made my way into work, and returned every evening in case we had any drunks or weirdos that might require a bit of muscle.

I soon learnt the true meaning of the saying 'They only come out at night'. Up until then I thought we had dealt with nearly every kind of creep. I'd certainly had my fair share of disgusting men over the years, but had never been more revolted than when the horrid schoolteacher visited us one night.

I was quite surprised when he turned up with a big wad of cash about an hour after phoning. During a lengthy telephone conversation he said he had a schoolgirl fantasy. This was one of the most common fantasies and we saw several punters a week, but there was something very disturbing about this one.

I was convinced he was going to walk when I told him how much the session with all three of us would cost, but he didn't hesitate and while swiftly counting out five hundred pounds told me what he wanted to do. I then left him in the dom-room in order to tell the girls.

Chloe said, 'He's horrid, Truly. Tell me we don't have to fuck him.'

'No, he wants a bit of school role play and relief.'

'Did you see his rotten teeth?' asked Alice.

And Chloe said, 'Yeah, and his breath stinks.'

'I know he's repulsive, but he's paid good money.'

Chloe asked, 'What exactly do we have to do?'

'He wants to be your schoolteacher and spank you a little bit for being naughty.'

Alice asked, 'What do you have to do?'

'Oh, I'm the headmistress,' I told her.

'That's good, cos you can make sure he doesn't smack us too hard,' Chloe said.

'Don't worry, he won't. Anyway, Carl's here.'

'Okay, come on, Alice, let's get changed.'

'While you're getting ready, I'll go start the session.'

Alice asked, 'Shall we wait outside the door till you call us?'

'Yeah.'

When I walked in I found him with his hand down his trousers and he didn't even stop what he was doing. He really was the most disgusting creature I'd ever seen. He reminded me of a medieval mad monk with his large bald patch and bulging eyes. Even his clothes resembled a monk's outfit: big long-sleeved baggy brown T-shirt and matching trousers, with a belt and a massive belly. I grinned and wondered how long it had been since he'd seen his cock.

'Where are the girls, headmistress?'

'They're waiting outside the door.'

'Call them in, please.'

'Come in, girls.'

'You know the reason you're here, don't you?'

Chloe and Alice were now so experienced at school role play they didn't have to be prompted, and Alice said, 'Yes, sir, we've been naughty, and we're here to be caned by the headmistress.'

'What have they been up to?' I asked.

And the punter said, 'They've been messing about in the sex education lesson.'

'Is this true, girls?'

'Yes, miss,' they said in unison.

'Alice, lift up your dress and bend over the desk,' I commanded.

And the perv shouted at Chloe, 'What are you giggling about, girl?' He was so aggressive I immediately became concerned that this was more than a game to him. 'I'll deal with you in a minute!' he shouted

Chloe's face turned very serious and from the look she gave me I could see she was genuinely scared. After glaring at Chloe for a moment he then turned his attention to me.

'Are you going to spank her or not, headmistress?'

I couldn't believe the creep. He was giving me the same menacing look. Without answering him I began to gently cane Alice and after a few strokes he stripped off and revealed his grotesque body. He must have been even fatter at some time in his life, because great long lengths of loose stretch-marked skin hung from his bottom, inner thighs and underarms. I would've felt sorry for him if he didn't have such a nasty nature.

Suddenly and without warning he grabbed Chloe by the hair and tried to force her to suck his dick. He was getting far too carried away, and if I wanted to avoid involving Carl I needed to take control of his game. If I didn't, we were in for trouble.

'Let me cane her before you teach her a lesson.'

Thankfully he let go of her, saying, 'Very well, headmistress. Give her a dozen strokes.'

As I was caning her he started to walk towards her backside. I knew what the bastard intended to do, I could see it in his face. Before he got a chance to stick his unprotected dick in poor Chloe I pushed her off the desk and onto the floor.

'Now get out of here and go back to your lessons, both of you!'

Chloe looked towards Alice who was standing in the far corner, well away from the guy, and said to her, 'Come on, Alice, let's go.'

The punter said, 'I haven't dismissed you yet, girls.'

I'd had enough of this creep and didn't care how much he'd paid. It was time to show him who was in charge.

I told the girls, 'Go downstairs and tell the headmaster I may need him to come upstairs.'

Chloe immediately got the message. She winked and said, 'Shall I tell him to come up right away?'

'No, tell him to wait till I shout out.'

As soon as the girls left the room, he demanded to know why I didn't allow him to have sex with Chloe and insisted I call her back in. After lying to him by saying we were strictly a flat for domination and didn't offer sexual services, he calmed down and asked very nicely if he could be relieved in some way. I didn't want to involve the girls for fear of him kicking off again, so I offered to relieve him at a ridiculously high price. Without questioning the amount he went over to his trousers and counted out one hundred and fifty pounds, passed it to me and laid down on the floor.

'Tell me the most disgusting thing you've done.'

I wanted to say that he was in fact the most disgusting thing I'd done. I knew better than to insult him though, so while I wanked him I talked about fisting and putting my tongue up bums.

After a minute or two he shouted, 'Wank me harder, I'm going to come.'

He was so noisy when he shot his load I thought people in the street would hear, even though we were on the third floor.

After showing the punter out, I went into the kitchen and found Chloe and Alice telling Carl about the session.

Chloe said to me, 'Thank God that creep's gone.'

'Never mind him, I think it's time to go home.'

Alice asked, 'Can we go, Truly?'

'Yeah sure.'

While the girls got changed I counted out the money and gave Carl a few notes. He was always reluctant to take it, but I insisted. After all, he was much too precious to be taken advantage of. Because Chloe was worried the punter might be waiting outside somewhere, Carl walked us to the underground.

I said to everyone, 'Have a good weekend. See you all on Monday.'

And Chloe said, 'Don't forget Stompy's coming on Monday.'

'That should be interesting,' I replied.

Alice said, 'Yeah, I can't wait, I'm going to crush him to death.'

Carl walked away shaking his head, saying, 'You lot are mad. See ya later.'

Chapter 34

I had a dreadful weekend. It all started with my partner spending most of the day chatting online to women. I became really infuriated when he denied flirting with them. I knew he was lying, because unbeknown to him I'd found his password a few weeks before written on a piece of paper and since then I'd been having a good look at what he was up to on the laptop in the London flat. I was surprised at how careless he was by not bothering to delete the conversations and emails.

Chloe suggested I flirt with him online to find out if it was harmless fun or if he was intending to go further. So with her help we created a couple of profiles with pictures of mature catalogue models and placed them on the sites he frequented. I was surprised that after only two days he made contact with both women. He began by saying how pretty they were, and how he wasn't in a relationship and was hoping to find someone serious. I was so angry after reading his bullshit I couldn't continue communicating with him online. Chloe and Alice both agreed he wasn't worth getting upset about.

But this particular time I just saw red when he lied to me, so much so that I slapped his face as hard as I could. When he asked why I'd hit him I stupidly confessed that two of the ladies he'd chatted with were in fact me. I told him if I'd continued it would've only been a matter of time before I managed to reel him in. Fortunately, the boys were out because he went ballistic. He grabbed me by the arms and threw me across the room. I landed badly, hitting my face on the skirting.

Consequently, we spent the rest of the day avoiding each other. My partner had once told me how he'd hung his ex-wife over the balcony of their flat by her ankles when he discovered she was having an affair. If that was true, I knew he was capable of anything if rattled, so that night I slept with one eye and ear open.

I woke up with a black eye and bruises shaped like handprints on my upper arms. I didn't want the boys to know the truth in case they confronted my partner, so I put a long-sleeved blouse on and told them I'd tripped over one of the dogs and hit my face on the table.

On my way into work I daydreamed about how life used to be for the boys and me before I'd met my partner. We were all so happy and free. I promised myself that one day soon I'd leave the controlling bastard, but if I wanted to walk away alive I would have to plan my escape very, very carefully.

The girls didn't need to guess how I'd sustained my bruises. I admitted that even though I'd come off worse, I felt pleased I had confronted him.

Chloe laughed and said, 'Do you realise every time he chats online now he's going to think twice about who he's talking to?'

'You must want to kill the bastard,' Alice said.

'I've been bloody close, that's for sure.'

'He's not worth serving the sentence for,' said Chloe. 'You need to leave him, Truly.'

'Yeah, I know. Anyway, let's not talk about him any more.'

Chloe then suggested, 'You could always jump on Stompy with me today and pretend it's him.'

'No thanks, I'll let you two youngens do that. It sounds a bit too energetic for my liking.'

We had a hectic morning, and by the afternoon I was so exhausted I was tempted to lie down on the bed, but it was gone three and Stompy was due at four, and Carl would be coming soon to collect some more cards. So while the girls were watching telly in the other room I counted out the cards. I was about halfway through when he texted to say he was at the door.

'Do us a favour, Alice, let Carl in.'

When he walked into the kitchen and saw me he said, 'What fucking pervert did that?'

'Don't panic, Carl, it wasn't a punter, it was my partner.'

'Fucking bastard. Do you want me to have a word with him?'

'No, don't worry. I'm okay.'

'Why do you stay with him?'

'I guess I learnt to take shit at an early age.'

'What do ya mean? You don't take any shit from punters.'

'That's different. I'm not emotionally involved with them.'

'Sorry to interrupt, Truly,' Chloe said, 'but Stompy's just texted. He's at Goodge Street Station, so he'll be here in five minutes.'

'Okay, you'd better get ready.'

'Did you remember to get a couple of bottles of wine for him?'

'Shit, I forgot.'

'I'll go get them for ya if you like,' said Carl.

'Thanks a lot, Carl. Here's twenty quid.'

Chloe told him, 'Don't bother getting anything too expensive. It's only to get him pissed so he'll spend more money here.'

'Okay, I'll go now before he's at the door.'

A few minutes after Carl left, the buzzer rang.

'Grab that, Chloe,' I said.

'Shall I go and let him in?'

'Yeah, please.'

I could hear Chloe giggling and chatting as they came up the stairs.

'Can we come in, Truly?'

Normally the kitchen was out of bounds to punters, but as he was an old regular of Chloe's I had no objection to him coming in for a few minutes until Carl got back. Chloe introduced me to Patrick before taking him upstairs to meet Alice. He was a rather strange-looking little man. His shape appeared disproportional, with a huge head and torso with skinny arms and legs, like the kind of figure a child makes out of Plasticine.

Carl got back with the wine and Chloe and Alice came into the kitchen. Chloe slapped a wad of notes on the table, smiled and said, 'He's going to stay for four hours, okay?' She then grabbed a glass and bottle of wine and they went back upstairs.

Carl and I thought we were in the middle of an earthquake when the light fittings above us started to shake violently. Judging by the loud thumps they must have been jumping off the bed onto him.

'Fucking hell, Truly, they're going to kill him if they keep that up for four hours.'

'Yeah, and Chloe told me he's got a huge hernia.'

'I'm not surprised if he likes that kind of treatment. Anyway, I'd better get going. Do ya want me back later?'

'No, don't worry. I'm going to close when Stompy leaves.'

After an hour the girls came downstairs. Chloe said it was thirsty work and they needed a tea and ciggie break.

'What's Stompy doing?'

'Oh, he's fine. He's got his wine.'

'Okay, so if any punters call, instead of losing money, one of you can pretend to have a break and do them in the dom-room.'

'Yeah, no problem,' Chloe said. 'I'll just turn the radio up a bit in the bedroom.'

Alice then said to me, 'Stompy wants you to come and see the show.'

'I'll come up in a bit.'

The smell in the bedroom was quite offensive: a mixture of belches and farts, the consequence of the girls jumping on him with such ferocity that he expelled the noxious fumes uncontrollably. As I watched I became increasingly concerned about his massive hernia. Alice seemed to be avoiding the bulge, but Chloe appeared to deliberately jump as if she were trying to burst it. I'd seen and done some disgusting things, but nothing had made me feel as repulsed as this fetish. The sick bastard didn't even seem to be enjoying himself; he looked really ill. I only hoped he wasn't going to throw up all over the room.

I decided I'd seen enough, so without saying anything I walked out and went back downstairs. For the last couple of hours Chloe entertained her punter while Alice assisted me with a couple of dom punters.

Stompy wasn't in any hurry to leave. Chloe had to remind him a few times that his time was up and I was in a hurry to lock up and go home. He finally got the hint and left. He was a little worse for wear, not only from the pounding he'd received, but the two bottles of wine must have taken effect when he stepped out into the fresh air. We watched from the window as he walked along the road and laughed as he swayed from side to side. At one point he lost his balance and nearly fell into the gutter.

Alice said, 'Serves him right for drinking so much.'

Chloe said, 'Yeah, he's such a greedy pig.'

We were getting ready to go home when Chloe received a text from Stompy thanking us all for giving him such a lovely time and wanting to know if he could spend his birthday with us the following Monday. This was really good news. Besides the endless new faces that came through the door each day, our list of regular wealthy punters was growing and we now had several long-stay ones visiting on a weekly basis.

Chapter 35

As predicted, the day got off to a good start. It was the end of the month and in the trade that meant punters with more than just throbbing cocks in their trousers; they also had cash in their pockets. Brooke was chosen for a two-hour dom-session and Alice had a visit from a regular who adored her and always tipped well.

Unfortunately, the afternoon took a turn for the worse when I opened the door to every brothel's most unwelcome visitor. We'd not long finished lunch and the girls were relaxing in the sitting room while I washed the dishes. The entry buzzer rang and when the guy spoke there was nothing in his voice to suggest anything alarming was about to happen. He simply said he'd rung earlier, so I pressed the release button to open the street door and went to let him in.

The moment I opened the door I was confronted by two uniformed policemen wielding a battering-ram. Before I got a chance to react they pushed past me, and to my horror there was a loud thudding on the stairs as four plain clothes, two of them women, came charging past.

I wasn't particularly surprised by the raid, more disappointed. After all, Carl had warned me from the start that it was only a question of time before my luck ran out. I just hadn't expected it to be quite so soon. I paused for a few seconds and took a couple of deep breaths before facing them.

One of the uniformed coppers stood in the hallway while I was led into the kitchen by the other PC. As we walked past the sitting room I could hear one of the female officers talking to the girls. She was speaking very politely and was not being at all aggressive or intimidating.

The reception I received was more like something out of an episode of The Sweeney. Their manner was extremely hostile, and from the moment I walked into the kitchen I was up against the other three plain clothes and was immediately bombarded with questions.

'Who are you? Do you run the flat? Are you the maid? Who collects the money?'

My head was reeling and my heart racing, but I knew I had to remain cool and calm or they'd eat me alive. If I were to come out of this unscathed somehow I needed to get hold of Andrew.

'Are you going to answer our questions or do we need to take you down to the station?'

'I'm sorry, but I need to go to the toilet first.'

'Okay, but a PC will be outside the door.'

Fortunately, I was in the habit of hiding my private mobile behind the back of some toilet rolls in the bathroom cabinet. I only hoped Andrew was available to answer my call.

'Oh thank God you've answered, Andrew.'

'What's the matter? Are you okay?'

'No. I've got six cops in the flat.' I began to calm down as I listened to Andrew's advice. Under no circumstances was I to admit to running or owning the flat, and until proved otherwise I just worked there as the maid. Before I got the chance to say anything back to him, the PC started banging on the door.

'What are you doing in there?'

Andrew said, 'You must go and answer their questions, but keep your answers short. I'll call you back in five minutes. Just keep calm. I'm here for you, okay?'

'Thank you, Andrew. I don't know what I'd do without you.'

'Who were you talking to in there?'

'My solicitor.'

'Why do you have a solicitor?'

'What do you mean? Doesn't everyone have a solicitor?'

'Not when you're just the maid.'

'I don't know what you mean. I only work here.'

'You still haven't told us who collects the money.'

I knew that if I pretended someone came to the flat to collect the money they would persist, so I said I met them in a café or pub and it wasn't always the same person, and I had no idea who the owner was.

The officer who was throwing all the questions at me seemed to be running out of patience and he started to raise his voice. At one point his face was so close to mine I felt his spit as he said, 'If you don't answer our questions, we'll take you down to the station.'

I was beginning to get really angry with his threats, but I knew he wanted me to bite and there was no way I was going to give him the satisfaction of marching me off in handcuffs.

I wasn't the only one having it rough. The kitchen door opened and Brooke was led through by one of the uniforms.

She said, 'About fucking time. You could have let me come and get a cigarette on my own.'

As she reached for her handbag he grabbed it and began to search it.

Brooke took hold of it and said, 'What do you think you're doing?'

'I'm having a look.'

'Well fuck off, unless you've got a warrant.'

'Are you married?'

The PC had noticed Brooke wore a wedding and engagement ring. Right then she probably wished she'd taken my advice when I'd told her a long time ago to take them off when she was working.

'Yeah, what's it got to do with you?'

'Does your husband know what you do?'

'No, why?'

'How can you go home and sleep with him when you've been sleeping with men for money?'

'How come you've got such an attitude? You should be more open-minded if you're working with the vice squad.'

Andrew's call couldn't have come soon enough. If things had continued between the officer and Brooke I could see us all being marched off to the police station.

'What's happening?' Andrew asked.

The officer who'd been firing most of the questions at me interrupted. 'Who are you talking to?'

Andrew clearly heard what he said and suggested I pass the phone over to him.

'My solicitor would like to have a word with you.'

The cop's voice was a mixture of restrained anger and frustration. From the one-sided conversation I understood that Andrew was asking if I was being treated okay and if I was under arrest, and if that were to happen he wanted to be informed. After reassuring Andrew that he would keep him up to speed with any changes he passed the phone back to me.

Andrew said, 'I don't think, at this stage, you're going to be arrested. They think you're the maid, so play dumb and I'll phone you back in five minutes.'

No sooner had I ended the call than I was subjected to more intimidation from the same officer. He shoved a piece of paper in front of me and said, 'You have to sign this.'

I was getting used to his behaviour by now and was beginning to relax, safe in the knowledge that I had Andrew on the other end of the phone.

'What's it for?'

'Just sign it.'

I smiled at him ever so sweetly and replied, 'I don't sign anything without my solicitor present.'

'Up until now you haven't done a bloody thing without your precious solicitor.'

After reading a couple of sentences it was quite clear what the paper was about, and there was no way I was going to sign it.

'Well, are you going to sign it here or are we going to have to take you down to the station?'

'Just a minute, I need to consult my solicitor.'

The officer could hardly contain his temper and his face was like a slapped arse as I rang Andrew yet again. After reading out the paper, word for word, Andrew said I was under no obligation to sign a document admitting to running a brothel, much to the cop's obvious frustration. I was still on the phone talking to Andrew when they all walked to the door, and he asked what was happening.

'I think they're leaving.'

'Okay, call me back.'

Before leaving, the two PCs collected up the cards that were stored in the sitting room. I wished I'd listened to Carl's advice when he told me to store the cards elsewhere. I felt like saying how petty and ridiculous they were, but I kept my mouth shut in case they changed their minds and arrested me. Finally they made their move, but not before Big Mouth made one more threat.

'We'll be back in six weeks, so make sure you're gone.'

I watched with relief as they drove off in a couple of unmarked cars in the direction of Conway Street. I wondered who they were going to visit next; maybe the flat in Cleveland Street run by a Chinese lady.

Alice asked, 'Are you okay, Truly?'

'Yeah, I'm coming up.'

Brooke reckoned we all needed a stiff drink to help us get over the shock. Luckily I kept a bottle of vodka in the fridge. After a few mouthfuls I felt calmer and the colour came back into the girls' cheeks. I don't think any of us had expected the police to be quite so unpleasant and bullying.

Brooke asked, 'What should we do now?'

'We'll have to close for a couple of days so I can get some more cards done.'

Brooke said to Alice, 'I can't understand why they were so nice to you and so fucking horrible to me and Truly.'

'It's because I'm foreign. They think someone's pimping me.'

'Well that's true,' Brooke said. 'Your husband pimps you, doesn't he?'

'He doesn't force me to do it.'

I then said to them, 'This is no time for an argument, you two. What did the policewoman say to you, Alice?'

'The silly bitch wanted to know if I was being forced to do this job.'

'What did you say?'

'I laughed and told her I loved dominating men, and that I probably earned more than her.'

'You're joking! Did you really say that?'

'Yes, why not? It's true.'

'Did you tell her I'm the boss?'

'She nearly did,' Brooke said.

'You're joking.'

'Don't worry, Truly. I told her I knew nothing because I'd only just started working here.'

When the girls went home I rang Carl and told him what had happened. He thought they probably weren't bluffing about getting me out, but first they needed to find out who my landlord was and then put pressure on him to have me evicted. Until then he advised me to make as much money as I could before they returned.

Even though the police visit had cast a shadow I was determined that the fun would continue. Andrew, on the other hand, wasn't happy with my decision and feared such a cavalier attitude towards the police would end in tears. Despite my choosing to ignore his advice to stop he promised to help me in any way he could, be it day or night.

Chapter 36

Three days later we opened for business and were in the middle of having coffee and croissants on the roof terrace when the phone rang. The Monthly Muncher, as we called him, had a habit of ringing at the same time every month. After exchanging a few pleasantries he got round to the obvious reason for calling.

I covered the speaker with my hand before asking the girls, 'The Monthly Muncher wants to know if anyone's on.'

'It's Chloe's turn this time.'

'Are you on, Chloe?'

'Yeah, I've just started. Tell him to come round in a couple of hours so my tampon's full.'

It was very difficult to keep a straight face because the girls were giggling so much, but somehow I managed to confirm that Chloe was able to accommodate his fancies and asked him to pop round for a nibble at twelve thirty.

While waiting for him to arrive we had a visit from one of our favourite wealthy men. He liked to spend a couple of hours having his face sat on by us. Normally face sitting invariably led to a tongue slipping up a fanny or backside, even though we strictly forbade it, especially when it involved all three of us, because of cross-contamination. But this punter was a pleasure because he had a fetish for tights and big knickers. With that amount of protection we were quite happy to sit on him for hours.

Chloe couldn't help herself. Whenever she sat on him she always told him this was the only time she really did get paid for sitting on the job. I don't know why, but hearing her say it as she bounced up and down on his face always made him come.

I left the girls to finish the session because I needed to let Carl in.

'Alright, Carl, how's it going?'

'Not bad. Are you okay?'

'Yeah, I am now.'

'Good, cos I was worried about how you'd cope with your first police visit.'

'To tell you the truth, it's business as usual.'

'Good, you mustn't let them scare you off. By the way, I noticed a bloke hanging around outside and he keeps looking at his watch.'

'Oh, it's not the police, it's only The Muncher. He's nearly always early. Hang on a minute, Carl, I need to get rid of the guy upstairs.'

Carl still had the same bemused expression on his face when I walked back into the kitchen followed by the girls.

Chloe said, 'I hope I've got time to eat before The Muncher gets here.'

The buzzer answered her question.

'Quick, Chloe, go upstairs while I let him in.'

Considering Carl had been in the business for over twenty years he was still keen to compare stories. After I told him about The Monthly Muncher, Alice and I listened in utter horror as he delighted in giving us the gory details of his account. Mr Crunchy Nut and Pooh Flakes was a regular visitor to most of the flats in the area. His favourite meal was cornflakes and warm milk topped with a couple of dollops of shit that he liked to have fed to him.

I had to admit that what I'd just heard made The Menstrual Muncher's appetite sound mild in comparison, and it only helped reinforce my policy of never allowing a punter to kiss me on the lips.

I thought the only threat I had to worry about was the police. That was until Alpha appeared on the scene again. It had been three weeks since the raid and we were busier than ever, particularly with the twenty-minute dom service. Carl reckoned the reason for the flat's popularity was because no other dominatrix in London offered a session for less than one hundred and fifty pounds, so whereas normally only wealthy men could afford it I'd made it possible for most men to try.

We were relaxing after an extremely busy morning when the buzzer rang and Chloe answered it. Instead of her usual excited response to a punter's arrival she had a very worried look on her face when she came back into the sitting room.

'What's the matter?' I asked.

'I don't know whether I've done the right thing, but I've just let Alpha in.'

'What the bloody hell is he doing here?'

'He didn't say.'

'Don't let him in the flat, Truly,' Alice said.

'I want to know what he wants. Don't worry, I'll put the chain on.'

By the time I got down the stairs he was banging on the door. I was glad I'd slipped the chain on because he wasn't alone. There were four more men squashed onto the small landing area and from what I could hear there were several others standing on the stairs.

'What do you want, Alpha?'

'I don't want any trouble, Truly, but I'm putting the cards out now.'

'I don't think so, that's Carl's job.'

'I'm not threatening you, but we've taken over.'

'Does Carl know?'

'He will soon.'

'Listen, Alpha, I gave you a chance and you were crap, so I suggest you go away.'

'You don't seem to understand, Truly. You don't have any choice.'

I closed the door in his face, put the bolts on, ran upstairs into the sitting room and phoned Carl.

Chloe asked, 'What's going on, Truly?'

'Alpha's trying to take over Carl's patch.'

Carl wasn't surprised when I told him I'd had a visit from Alpha and his heavies. He'd received several calls, and one independent woman even rang the police because he was refusing to leave the premises until she agreed to give him money and cards. It was only when she started talking to the police that he scarpered. Carl didn't believe in bullying women and for that reason he had rounded up his men and they were looking for Alpha. I had no doubt about his intentions. The anger in his voice was unmistakable. Carl never did tell me the outcome, but Alpha never darkened my door again.

Walkers, as we referred to them in the trade, were an accepted part of the job, but when a particular little man paid us a third visit I felt it was time to teach him a lesson. On two previous occasions I had introduced him to the girls, and after having a good ogle he made an excuse to leave. This time I recognised him the moment I opened the door. If there really was a way a pervert was supposed to look then this one certainly would have got the part. He was short and chubby, in his early fifties, with balding dark hair and wore thick-lens glasses. His beige suit was crumpled and his shirt probably started out being white but was now a nasty greyish colour, which clashed with his brown and cream striped tie.

I led him up the stairs and left him in the bedroom while I went back down to get the girls, who were in the kitchen having tea with Carl.

'Guess who's here, girls?'

Chloe asked, 'Who?'

'It's the little fat walker, with the thick glasses.'

'Oh, not again,' Alice moaned. 'He was here the other week.'

And Chloe said, 'He only comes here to look.'

I told them, 'Well this time he's going to get more than a look.'

'Do you want me to see him out?'

'No thanks, Carl, I'm going to enjoy this one.'

'Okay, Truly, but I'm going to stay in case you need me.'

'Come on, girls, let's have some fun.'

When we walked into the bedroom the guy had his hand down his pants. He'd obviously been playing with his cock because it was bulging prominently through his trousers. I introduced him to Chloe and Alice, and instead of leaving the room so they could have a little chat in private I asked them to leave.

I then asked him, 'Now tell me, what excuse have you got lined up this time?'

His expression changed from excitement to fear in an instant and he said, 'What are you on about?'

'Well, let me explain. This is your third time of having a look and a wank at our expense, so I suggest you leave before I introduce you to my friend. He's sitting downstairs and I know he's dying to meet you.'

I didn't need to tell him twice because he made a dash out of the bedroom, and as he descended the two flights of stairs I couldn't help assisting his fat arse on its journey with my stiletto boots. By the time he reached the door I must have kicked his backside a dozen times. Needless to say the girls had witnessed his swift departure and were collapsed on the hallway floor in fits of laughter. I walked into the kitchen to find Carl laughing.

'Truly, you really are a gutsy lady.'

'Do you think so?'

'Yeah, I couldn't help having a look at you in action.'

'I didn't see you.'

'No, you were too busy kicking his arse.'

'I don't think he'll come back.'

'I'd put money on that.'

Chapter 37

I hated having to sack girls, but Judy gave me no option. For the previous two weeks she'd been moody and antisocial towards the other girls. She'd even phoned Brooke to have a bitch and moan about the favouritism that went on in the flat. Brooke tried to explain to her that she thought she was wrong and that I tried to treat all the girls equally, but it made no difference. The amount of puff and coke she did made her paranoid and unable to see things clearly.

So when I left her for twenty minutes to go to the bank and came back to find her fast asleep on the sitting room floor with a joint in her hand and a burn mark on the carpet, I knew she was a risk I couldn't afford. I hardly dared think what might happen if she were at the flat when the police paid us another visit. I woke her up and explained I wasn't prepared to put up with her doing drugs at work, and unless she was able to give them up I had no option but to ask her to leave.

Carl did his best to make me feel better when he called in about an hour after she'd left.

'What's the matter, Truly? You look stressed.'

'I've just had to sack Judy for smoking weed in the flat.'

'You had to do it. You can't take the risk when you've got the police hanging around the place.'

'I know, but I still feel shit about it.'

'Most people think running a knocking-shop is easy money, but it's hard, and the one running it has to be even harder cos unfortunately, girls in this business see kindness as a weakness and they will soon bring you down if you show it.'

I didn't have time to dwell on Judy for long, as I was far too busy flogging an overweight middle-aged woman while her impotent partner watched. When I took the call she explained she wanted to be punished by a dominatrix with her partner present. I quoted an exorbitant tribute because I thought it was a hoax, so when they turned up twenty minutes later I was very surprised.

Once in the dom-room she stood silently while her partner said he wanted me to cane her backside and fuck her with any toys I wished. I couldn't help wondering why a middle-aged woman would want to be subjected to this kind of treatment by a complete stranger. I reminded myself that I wasn't being paid to analyse her, and from what I could see she wasn't being forced to do something she didn't want to do so I may as well relish the experience.

I began the session by ordering them to strip off. As they stood before me I couldn't quite decide which body was the most unfortunate. He was pigeon-chested, puny and without a trace of muscle tone, while she was short and fat, rather like a barrel, her tits were saggy and her bottom and thighs had the texture of orange peel.

I told him to sit in the far corner of the room while I tied her to the Saint Andrew's cross and then to count in time to each stroke. Her bottom wobbled like a big pink blancmange as I brought the cane down on it, strike after strike, and as I paused and glanced over at him he nodded for me to continue. Even though I was a dominatrix it didn't give me the right to thrash someone against their wishes, so before bringing the cane down on her again I whispered in her ear, 'Do you want me to continue?'

'Yes, it excites him.'

I wasn't surprised by her reply, as it wasn't the first time I'd encountered a woman indulging her partner's sexual fantasies at her own expense. I once visited a couple who wanted me to participate in a threesome. When the guy rang to make the booking he assured me his girlfriend wanted the session, but when I turned up it was a different story. She looked as if she'd been crying and I got the impression she was merely going through the motions to please him. A threesome is fine if there's no emotional involvement, but when in a relationship it can go disastrously wrong.

After a few more strokes, despite him wanting me to continue thrashing the poor bitch, I knew it was time to stop because the weal marks were bleeding. That wasn't the only thing concerning me. Up until then he hadn't managed to get hard and I began to wonder if he had an erection problem. Maybe it was her way of trying to breathe some life into his cock. He finally began to wank as he watched me buckle on a strap-on, and after slipping on a condom I walked over to her and squirted a small amount of lubricant onto my index finger. She let out gentle moans as I rubbed it over the entrance to her fanny. After releasing her from the cross I commanded her to get on all fours.

It certainly didn't take long for her to show her appreciation. After a few thrusts of the rubber cock she let out the unmistakable moans of a woman having an orgasm. I continued to please her for a bit longer; after all, judging by her partner's lifeless cock it was the best seeing to she'd had in a long time. I was getting tired of waiting for him to get hard, so I decided to leave them to their own devices for the last ten minutes of the session. Leaving the room I told him to finish her off in any way he wanted and to come downstairs when they were dressed and ready to leave.

Six weeks had passed since the police visit and everyone was on tenterhooks waiting for them to bang on the door again. I did my best to put on a brave face in front of the girls, but unbeknown to them my health was beginning to suffer and my palpitations were worse than ever. To make matters worse my partner had fallen out with my uncle and had packed his job in. It was easy for my cardiologist to recommend I listen to the warning signs my body was giving out and change my lifestyle, but I didn't have the luxury of a supportive partner, be it financially or emotionally, so unless I wanted to go downhill again I saw no option but to carry on.

One of the many advantages of being a dominatrix was that if I was feeling under pressure or pissed off about something, I could vent it out on a punter. I got the opportunity to do just that one morning shortly after having an argument with my partner on the phone. Chloe and Alice were about half an hour into a session with a guy that wanted cock and ball torture when they asked for my assistance. Chloe came into the kitchen looking very flushed and anxious.

'Can you come up and help us, Truly? The perv's complaining.'

'What's the problem?'

'He reckons we're not severe enough.'

'What have you done to him?'

'Oh the usual, hot wax and electrics.'

'Okay, I'll be up in a minute.'

When I walked in the guy was tied to the Saint Andrew's cross. The moment he clapped eyes on me he began to complain about the treatment and how he felt the girls were far too timid to be mistresses. I let him finish having his moan about them and before he got a chance to say anything else I grabbed a ball gag from the shelf, shoved it in his mouth and buckled it so tight he nearly choked.

'Have you heard the old saying, girls: silence is golden? Well, now you know what granny meant when she said it.'

They looked on and nodded in approval as I swiftly tied his balls up with a length of cord. First I placed it round his neck so each end hung equally down to just a few inches below the level of his balls. After separating them in the scrotum I tied the cord around one ball and then pulled on the other end until he was trembling with pain.

After tying the other ball I looked into his eyes and whispered, 'Comfortable, I trust?'

What I did next brought tears to his eyes, and I must admit I thoroughly enjoyed watching him suffer. I lit a candle, and instead of the usual punishment of dribbling hot wax on his genitals I held the candle underneath so the flame touched his scrotum. Even though his mouth was full I could make out he was telling me to stop. I grinned and thought, *this punter does have a boiling point when it comes to cock and ball torture, and he's obviously reached it now I've turned up the heat.* The smell of burning flesh and pubic hair quickly filled the air and he began to squirm and stand on his tiptoes to avoid the flame.

After several seconds I blew out the candle, and while removing the ball gag I looked him in the eyes and dared him to complain.

He replied in a pathetic tone, 'I'm sorry, mistress, I'm not fit to serve you.'

I sniggered and said, 'Now, before I decide to cut your balls off and nail them to the wall as a trophy, I recommend you get dressed quickly and go.'

After he left I suggested to the girls we eat out at the café on the corner. This was our favoured place; not only was the food delicious but it was also close enough for us to watch if any punters turned up. We were enjoying eating lunch outside in the sun when Carl came along. I could tell something was up by the worried look on his face.

'Sorry to interrupt your lunch, Truly, but can I have a word?'

'Yeah, sure.'

I left the girls to finish their lunch while Carl and I walked back to the flat so we could talk in private.

'I thought you'd better know the police closed two flats this morning.'

'Shit. Where?'

'Cleveland and Conway Streets.'

'You're joking? They're just around the corner.'

'Yeah, and they've been going for years.'

'How did they manage to close them?'

'They've obviously been putting pressure on the landlords.'

'I don't think I've got long.'

Carl didn't comment, he merely shrugged his shoulders in a nonchalant manner. I wasn't surprised by his response. After all, he must have seen more flats close than he'd had hot dinners, and even though I was sure he felt genuine affection for me I was just another working girl turned madam.

The afternoon dragged by with not a punter in sight. I know it was irrational thinking, but it was almost as though they'd got wind of the closure of flats and were staying away for fear of the police catching them on the premises.

At seven o'clock I decided to call it a day and we were getting ready to go home when I received a call from Spanker. He was a regular who liked to spank the girls' bottoms, and even though he was a highly strung, nervous kind of character he never hurt them.

He arrived in his usual state of excitement and almost knocked me over in his rush to get past me and up the stairs. As I followed him up I smiled as a friend's saying popped into my head: 'Have dick will travel'. She was absolutely right. The poor things seemed unable to think of anything else when their cocks were bothering them.

After spanking the girls and wanking he left in the same hasty manner. About twenty minutes later, when Alice and Chloe were busy with another late punter, Spanker rang again and said he'd left his BlackBerry behind. He must have thought I was some kind of crazy woman. It was only when I went into the dom-room while the session was going on and asked the girls if they'd seen a bag of blackberries lying around that I understood why he'd been so cross when I'd said, 'Maybe Chloe's eaten them.'

The girls and the man looked at me and began to laugh.

Chloe said, 'Truly, don't you know what a BlackBerry is?'

'Of course I do.'

'You silly cow! He's not talking about fruit, it's a smartphone.'

'Well why didn't the silly prat say so?' I replied angrily.

As I closed the door and walked back down the stairs I could hear all three of them roaring with laughter.

Chapter 38

I had no one to blame but myself as I sat outside the café on the corner of Warren Street. I was disguised in a blue headscarf and sunglasses I'd bought from a stall outside Goodge Street Station after receiving a frantic phone call from Chloe saying the police were raiding the flat and had thrown them out. What the fuck was I thinking of? I should never have given the girls the responsibility of opening the flat, no matter how much I needed some time off.

While sipping a coffee and trying to look inconspicuous I rang Andrew, and as always he was calm and professional. He advised me to stay clear of the premises until I was sure the police had gone. He nearly had kittens when I told him I had a clear view of the flat from where I was sitting.

After laughing and explaining I was in disguise, he began to calm down and said, 'You amaze me how you always manage to bring humour into the bleakest moments.'

The seriousness of the situation was brought back to me in a flash as I watched the police come out of the flat and pile into three unmarked cars. I recognised two of the cops from the first raid.

I told Andrew, 'They're leaving.'

'Listen to me. Don't go in the flat.'

'But I need to know what they've done.'

'If you must go in, wait for an hour before you do and leave as quickly as you can.'

I couldn't believe the state of the flat. It looked as though I'd had a robbery. The bastards had gone crazy. The contents of the kitchen drawers had been turned out and thrown onto the floor; the mattress had been turned up and tossed against the wall; everything in the dom-room had been ransacked; and my lovely antique school clock was lying face down on the floor with the glass smashed.

I needed to get out of the flat fast. Not only was the threat of the police returning a strong possibility, I felt sick and exhausted, and all I wanted to do was go somewhere quiet and batten down the hatches until the storm blew over. But that was wishful thinking, because Alice rang as I was on my way home with news that sealed my fate. Before throwing the girls out the police had been very heavy handed with Chloe and threatened to notify her family if she didn't sign the paperwork admitting the flat was used as a brothel. Although clearly a bluff, as they had no powers to do that when someone is of age, their intimidating tactics were more than Chloe could handle, and despite Alice telling her not to sign anything the police got their way. Armed with the evidence, all they had to do now was present it to my landlord.

As for my hefty deposit on the flat, I figured I might as well kiss that goodbye; there was little chance of getting it back when the landlord found out what had been going on. It was hard enough to get a deposit back at the best of times—landlords have a way of finding reasons for deducting money.

What I really needed to do, if I had the guts, was to work the flat for another week. At least that way I could earn the deposit back. After spending a couple of days worrying that the police were going to knock on the door of my home address and arrest me, I returned to work with a vengeance. Fortunately, since the last raid I'd learnt my lesson and had hidden the cards in the little shed on the roof. Luckily the police didn't search the roof terrace.

I might have been defeated by the police, but I was determined our last week was going to be the most profitable ever. Sadly, Chloe had been too traumatised by the ordeal and she decided not to return to work in the sex industry for the time being. Fortunately, Alice was brave enough and agreed to join me.

So once again I assumed the role of a dominatrix, only this time my anger was fuelled by my hatred towards the police and the draconian English laws on prostitution they enforce. We worked so hard raking in as much money as we could and not one punter was turned away, no matter how tired we were of looking at cocks, balls and smelly bums.

It was hardly surprising after what we'd been through that we conned and fleeced our very last customer. It was his fault really. He should never have turned up at a knocking-shop drunk and flashing a huge wallet full of cash. He was an irresistible target! I began by helping myself to his wallet in front of his very eyes, and after thoughtfully leaving him with twenty pounds to get home we began.

The session was meant to be for two hours, but after forty-five minutes of fucking him with a strap-on and burning his nipples with a cigarette, his eyes began to roll and he was looking a little worse for wear. This was more than likely from all the drink he'd consumed rather than our treatment. It was at that point that I seized the opportunity to get rid of him early.

I ordered Alice to blindfold him and tie him to the Saint Andrew's cross. He only just managed to stand as she buckled the wrist and ankle straps. After a few minutes of silence I tiptoed over to the school clock, which amazingly still worked despite having been flung across the room, and advanced the hand by an hour. I thought, *what the hell?* Thanks to the police I wasn't going to see this customer again.

My time was up, and so was his!

.

Lightning Source UK Ltd.
Milton Keynes UK
UKOW052002171211

183967UK00001B/18/P